PRAISE FOR GOOD OF ALL

"Matthew Daniels' idea of establishing a website and social networking movement seems to me important and timely. I have known Matt Daniels for many years and have been most impressed with his dedication, intelligence and the breadth of his organizational efforts. As everyone knows, the extraordinary power of the web played no small role in bringing about the collapse of totalitarian regimes in Eastern Europe and it is hard to imagine a successful human rights movement today that does not harness that power."
—Amb. Mary Ann Glendon, Professor of Law, Harvard University

○

"I have known Matt Daniels for several years from his work highlighting our nation's uniformed heroes through the *Great Americans* website and videos. I'm delighted to hear of his most recent work with Good of All. Matt understands the direct tie between freedom and national security. His efforts in developing a global human liberty campaign speak volumes about the vision that he brings to this most important issue."
—General Peter Pace (Retired), Former Chairman of the Joint Chiefs of Staff

○

"This Good of All educational campaign highlights the fact that the principles of the Universal Declaration can provide a common framework for freedom in our increasingly diverse and digitally mediated society."
—Nazir Afzal, OBE, Former Chief Crown Prosecutor, United Kingdom

"Legal equality for women is a fundamental human right and an important principle that furthers both human potential and social prosperity. So I am delighted that Brunel University Law School has entered into a partnership with the US charity Good of All to develop a centre for research into this area."

—Dominic Grieve, QC, Attorney General for England and Wales

○

"The Universal Declaration can serve as a Magna Carta for the Digital Age by providing a path for people around the world to unite through the global community of the Internet. This Good of All effort will promote a fuller digital expression of such universal rights as freedom of speech, association and privacy."

—Charles Falconer, Former Lord Chancellor of the United Kingdom

HUMAN LIBERTY 2.0

ADVANCING UNIVERSAL RIGHTS
IN THE DIGITAL AGE

MATTHEW DANIELS, JD, PHD

Post Hill
PRESS

A POST HILL PRESS BOOK
ISBN: 978-1-64293-100-6
ISBN (eBook): 978-1-64293-101-3

Human Liberty 2.0:
Advancing Universal Rights in the Digital Age
© 2019 by Matthew Daniels, JD, PhD
All Rights Reserved

Cover Design by Cody Corcoran

Post Hill Press
New York • Nashville
posthillpress.com

Published in the United States of America

TABLE OF CONTENTS

I

THE DEMOCRATIZATION OF RIGHTS IN THE DIGITAL AGE

II

DIGITAL HUMANITARIANS: THE UNSUNG HEROES OF *HUMAN LIBERTY 2.0*

PREFACE

NAZIR AFZAL, ORDER OF THE
BRITISH EMPIRE

As someone who has prosecuted cases involving the abuse of the internet—from violent extremist recruitment to online grooming—I know from experience that digital and social media can be used for destructive purposes. But this book is a celebration of the opposite.

The stories in this book illustrate how many in our time are using digital and social media to reach out across boundaries of culture and geography to advance the universal rights that are the birthright of all humanity. As such, this book series offers an expanding compendium of the largely unsung heroes and heroines of the Digital Age.

While the examples are too numerous to recount in the context of a short preface, consider how one simple digital tool (YouTube) has given ordinary people a tool to challenge everything from driving bans in Saudi Arabia to compulsory hijabs in Iran to police violence in Brazil.

Of course, such abuses have been a fact of life for many around the world for centuries. But this book speaks of the rise of a new collective global conscience that increasingly finds such oppression incompatible with civilization. Indeed, a central purpose of this book is to help encourage a movement of people in every country who regard the fundamental rights of others as a cause worthy of protection.

I often say that giving someone a cause to live for is far better than trying to prevent them from finding a cause to die for. The cause of advancing universal rights in the Digital Age is precisely such a cause.

Nazir Afzal, Order of the British Empire (OBE)
Former Chief Crown Prosecutor England & Wales
Former Chief Executive of the UK Police & Crime Commissioners

FOREWORD

ADMIRAL JAMES G. STAVRIDIS, FORMER

DEAN OF THE FLETCHER SCHOOL OF LAW

& DIPLOMACY

For more than a decade, a spreading global contagion of oppression has caused setbacks in human rights, of which the terror group ISIS—the so-called Islamic State of Iraq and Syria—is only the latest symptom. While no effective treatment has been developed for Ebola, a serum against its virulent moral and ideological counterparts emerged from the ashes of World War II.

That vaccine is embodied in the 1948 Universal Declaration of Human Rights, which former United Nations Secretary-General Boutros Boutros-Ghali called, "the quintessential values through which we affirm together that we are a single human community."

The breakthrough vision at the core of the Declaration is a call to ordinary men and women to unite in promoting the freedoms essential to realize fully our common humanity. It presumes that ordinary people will always have a greater stake in their own freedom than those in power.

The Declaration speaks of freedom of conscience, speech, property, and privacy. It condemns slavery, torture, and discrimination. It respects the dignity and worth of every human as equal, regardless of race, nationality, or gender.

Although a powerful and elegant expression our common birthright, the Declaration was arguably fifty years ahead of its time. This "good-idea virus" needed the Web to connect the ordinary people whom it seeks to protect. Equally important, it required a generation to come of age with the technology itself: "digital natives" who will communicate across boundaries in ways we cannot now even imagine. Only then could this historic expression of universal human rights become a meaningful social reality.

While the Declaration is already the most translated document in history, the internet has created an opportunity to disseminate and promote its vision of universal rights through the world's first nearly-universal communications medium. The emergence of a more globally conscious and interconnected generation of digital natives raised on the internet—especially in those parts of the world where ordinary people are resisting tyranny—has made it possible to inoculate more people than ever before with the inspiring truths of human freedom.

Liberty is an addictive drug. As Machiavelli warned in *The Prince*, "He who becomes master of a city accustomed to freedom and does not destroy it, may expect to be destroyed by it." Freedom itself is a powerful weapon against tyranny.

Throughout history there have been times when great ideas and technological advances converged with profound implications. We are again at such a time, and the task before us now is to ensure that the most potent ideals of human freedom are organically embraced by a new generation of digital natives across the globe. This, more than any weapons system, is our best hope for promoting and securing international peace and security.

Yet even in the face of this potential, American foreign policy and military leaders have devoted so much more energy and resources to hard power weaponry. They have put more faith in the power of killer drones than in life-giving ideals.

It has been an expensive miscalculation for those of us who must pay the bills while we watch ISIS advance. As General Myers, the former Chairman of the Joint Chiefs of Staff, has observed, "Every dollar spent on the soft power of ideas is worth one hundred in hard power." And the digitally-mediated barbarism of YouTube beheadings is a horrifying warning that technology can be used for good or evil.

Movements like ISIS are effective in their use of digital and social media, including the employment of very sophisticated and effective global online recruiting strategy. For the sake of all humanity, it is imperative that we turn that situation around and use the same technological advances at our fingertips to spread the good-idea virus of freedom and of universal rights to inoculate more hearts and minds against such destructive movements.

In the years ahead, our nation must focus more of our efforts on soft power. Our government should invest the funds needed to launch ten good ideas for every Tomahawk missile we fire. But the independent voice of the private sector is especially important in an era when public trust in political leaders and governments has reached a modern low ebb. So, the resources of the private sector should be harnessed to develop soft power networks and strategies that can help to soften the ground for freedom worldwide.

Ideas matter, and disseminating the timeless ideals of freedom to digital natives is the vital security imperative of our time. In the Digital Age, information truly is power—a new form of digital soft power that will be increasingly important to global freedom and security in the years ahead. The time has come to embrace its full potential as a force for good.

Admiral James G. Stavridis
Former Dean, Fletcher School of Law & Diplomacy,
Tufts University
United States Navy, Retired
Supreme Allied Commander, NATO (2009–13)

—————— I ——————

THE DEMOCRATIZATION OF RIGHTS IN THE DIGITAL AGE

CHAPTER 1

A DREAM BORN FROM A NIGHTMARE

Many of humanity's greatest dreams are born from the stuff of nightmares.

At the core of the *Human Liberty 2.0* revolution happening all around us is a collective human dream—a dream that will not die in spite of recurring episodes of war and genocide. It is a dream of a world where our shared humanity is more important than the superficial differences that can be used as a pretext for violence and oppression.

It is a dream where every person lives in freedom and enjoys human rights as enshrined in the Universal Declaration of Human Rights. Many do not share this dream of universal rights. Some people are militantly opposed to it. But the dream has a deep appeal because it is rooted in the timeless truth of our common human dignity.

Although our world is still ravaged by racism, cruelty, and violence, the advent of the Digital Age has made it harder to ignore the suffering and needs of others simply because they don't look like us, don't speak our language, or live in another part of the world.

This book series celebrates those whose lives embody a rising global awareness of our common humanity and a desire to promote the fundamental rights and well-being of other human beings as an investment in a better future for us all. They are the living expression of the dream of universal rights.

We begin to fulfill our potential as human beings when we seek to live for more than ourselves. Some people live their entire lives without coming to this realization. But I am convinced that all the great souls of history have come to this same timeless truth sooner or later. For example, in Dr. Martin Luther King Jr.'s last speech before his assassination, he invoked the famous example of the Good Samaritan. He called upon his audience to practice similar "dangerous unselfishness" toward those in need—particularly the weakest, the most vulnerable, and the most marginalized. Of course, anyone who understands the power of Dr. King's life and work will understand the hidden irony in this phrase— since a lifetime of selfishness can actually prove far more dangerous to our humanity in the end than a life of compassion and mercy.

My journey toward this realization came in the form of a nightmare that was rooted in my experience growing up in poverty in New York's Spanish Harlem. As a child, my precinct on the Upper West Side of New York City had the highest rate of violent crime in Manhattan. In fact, my family ended up on welfare after my mother, who was working as a single mom to support us, got off at a secluded bus stop after work and was assaulted by four men. They left her with a broken back and a lifelong disability. Her injuries were compounded by deep depression in the aftermath of the assault—a condition that she self-medicated with alcohol, contributing to her early death.

In my case, I was robbed more times than I can count—sometimes at knifepoint and several times at gunpoint—in the process of simply trying to get to and from school each day. In one case, I was kicked backward down a two-story escalator from an elevated subway station by two older teens who then followed me down and robbed me at the bottom. At the time, the thing that saved me was my school knapsack. It had slid up my back and provided a cushion for my head as I tumbled backward down the escalator banging my head on every step.

In fact, the trip through my neighborhood to school was so dangerous that I used to lie awake at night planning my route to and from school the next day. The goal was to try to make it through the danger zones in my neighborhood without getting mugged or assaulted. I would carefully plan out in my mind each street crossing with an eye toward stores where I might take refuge if something happened along the way.

Of course, the notion of receiving any help from law enforcement was not something that local residents ever considered; everyone knew that the police would only come into our neighborhood if there was a body in the street. We used to call it the "blood in the street" rule since calling the police simply to report a fight or even gunshots was as ineffective as calling about a barking dog. There needed to be an actual body in the street—and often there was.

In my building, stabbings were common in our lobby and elevator. I remember one time when a man followed a woman into the elevator of our building to rape her. When she screamed, he slashed her throat with a knife from ear to ear. Afterward, even though they cleaned the huge pool of blood off of the elevator floor, you could still see the dried blood in the corners. I would stare at her dried blood every morning on my way to school, hoping it would be gone by the next day. But the victim's dark red bloodstains remained visible there for weeks after she died.

Shootings were less common, but they still occurred relatively frequently. I remember seeing a drug dispute on the corner of our block escalate into a shooting. Since it was winter, the victim was wearing a puffy down coat as he stood on the corner talking to someone in a car. When the person in the car pulled a gun, the man ran, but he was shot multiple times as he tried to escape. Each bullet that hit him produced a puff of down that burst into the air following the trajectory of each bullet as it passed through his body. It was almost a comical sight—like watching someone shoot a pillow with a handgun—except that the victim could not outrun the bullets passing through his body. He made it about ten yards before he bled to death on our street.

Late at night, robberies were especially common because Riverside Park, which runs along the Hudson River, became a kind of ambush point and escape route for people looking for victims. One winter evening, I remember hearing a man's panicked voice screaming in the courtyard of our building, followed by several shots. Later that night the police took away the body of the person who had been mugged by an armed assailant who emerged from the shadows of the park across the street and ambushed him on his way home.

I never saw the actual body of the victim, but his screams and cries for help echoed in my mind all night. The next day, when I got up to go to school, I was confronted with a sight that was emblazoned deeply in my consciousness for many years. Because it was wintertime, the victim's blood had frozen on the sidewalk outside of our building. When I emerged from the lobby, I saw the elderly wife of my building superintendent using a stiff short-bristle broom and a bucket of hot water to try to scrub it off of the pavement. Her back was facing me as I walked outside. All I could do for several moments was stare at the image of this old woman stooped over a pool of frozen blood, with the steam from the hot water rising into the cold winter air. It struck me that this was all that remained of the nameless person whose screams I had heard the night before.

If you are killed or seriously injured on the streets of New York, an ambulance will take away your body after the police investigate the scene. But there is no city department or agency responsible for cleaning up your blood. As a result, depending on how you die, a part of you can be left on the sidewalk for people to stare at and walk around long after you are gone. For religious reasons, Orthodox Jews have special permission from New York City to use a jackhammer and break up any pavement stained with the blood of their community members, so that they can bury the victim with any traces of their blood. But for the rest of us, our blood remains where it was spilled. The same thing happened with respect to the woman who died in our elevator—leaving only the stain of her dried blood as a memorial to her death.

But on that cold winter morning, something about this grim sight made such a profound impression on me that it became a recurring nightmare that haunted me for years. In the nightmare, I emerge from my building to see the sight of my superintendent's wife quietly scrubbing the pavement. As I watch the steam rise from the warm water in her bucket and on the ground, I ask her, "Whose blood is this?" but she continues scrubbing silently. She does not even seem to know that I am there.

In the nightmare, I feel invisible and helpless. I have a burning desire to know the name of the person who died. It seems horrible not to know. But no matter how much I ask, the woman will not answer me or even acknowledge my presence.

Finally, in anguish, I walk closer to her. I begin to reach out to touch the old woman's shoulder, asking her again, "Whose blood is this? Who died here?" But the moment I start to move, she turns around and says, "You!"

Then I wake up. Her voice is ringing in my ears, telling me that I am the one who died.

Night after night. It is always the *same* nightmare with the *same* ending. It is always followed by the same tight knot in my stomach as I stare at the ceiling wondering what the nightmare means and why it will not go away.

For years, this nightmare haunted me. After working my way through a series of public schools in New York City, where I was usually one of the only white kids in the school, I received a full scholarship to Dartmouth College in New Hampshire. Dartmouth is arguably the most remote and safest Ivy League campus in America. It is harder to think of a place more different from my neighborhood. For me, going to Dartmouth was the closest I had ever come to traveling to another planet. But the nightmare still followed me there.

As a freshman, I can vividly remember the nightmare routinely waking me up in the middle of the night. And it was always the *same* nightmare with the *same* disturbing ending. Week after week, I would sit up terrified in bed, only to hear the sound of chirping crickets and remember that I was hundreds of miles from New York City. It seemed bizarre that the nightmare had followed me to a place where you could probably fall asleep on the campus green with a pile of money for a pillow and no one would even think to bother you.

After a great deal of soul-searching, I finally realized that part of the meaning of this nightmare was a calling. The nightmare was a call for me to see the suffering of others as if I *myself* was suffering. Of course, this sort of deep empathy is something that good parents may feel with respect to their own children. It is an entirely different matter to feel such empathy for a total stranger. And my personality is such that I am not an empathetic person by nature. But the nightmare was a message to me to try to live differently. The nightmare was a call for me to understand a timeless truth: *No man (or woman) is an island...and the suffering of others should concern us as much as our own suffering.* Their suffering and death diminishes us if we ignore it. To deny that reality is to deny your own humanity.

This book was written in an attempt to honor those in our day who have discovered this same timeless truth and tried to put it into action.

The great souls of every age are all imperfect people who still dare to dream and sometimes live beyond the limitations of their own frailty and failings. The men and women whose stories are captured in this book series embody the reality of our shared humanity.

In my case, the nameless person who died in front of my building that night became a lifelong symbol for me of all the nameless, faceless victims of violence and suffering in our world. Just as I never saw the body of the person who died that winter night, we will never personally see most of the victims of human rights abuses in our world. But we must never close our ears or deaden our conscience to their tears, their cries, or their blood.

CHAPTER 2

HARNESSING THE POTENTIAL OF OUR SHARED HUMANITY

No man is an island, . . .

Any man's death diminishes me,

Because I am involved in mankind;

and therefore never send to know for whom the bell tolls;

It tolls for thee.

—John Donne (1572–1631)
Meditation XVII
Devotions upon Emergent Occasions

I had never before heard the breathtaking sound of bells ringing out across an entire city.

It was April 19, 2013, and all of Warsaw's bell towers seemed to be echoing across both the rooftops and the ages John Donne's ancient poetic insight about our common humanity. The tolling bells commemorated the seventieth anniversary of the Warsaw Ghetto Uprising and the sacrifices of those who tried to resist the Nazi regime's massacre of the largest Jewish population in Europe.[1] The sound sent shivers down my spine as the realization set in that, by extension, those bells were also mourning the tragedy of Auschwitz and the many other death camps built by the Third Reich across Poland. As the victims of the Holocaust were countless, so were the bells ringing in their memory.

Yet the idea that was born in my mind that day was not one of despair. It was an idea conceived in hope.

Bells were a simple communications technology that John Donne's generation employed to help people feel the connection we share because of our common humanity. For centuries, bells have been rung in high places in both the East and the West to call people to an awareness above the level of mere survival and selfish existence. So it seemed appropriate that the ancient sound of bells would call to my mind a universal truth about the reality of our shared human dignity.

It was there, amidst the unforgettable sound of those bells ringing over a land that had seen so much brutality and bloodshed, where I realized that we now live in a very different age—a Digital Age in which people can do more in the face of oppression than ever before, both to expose tyranny and abuses and to unite with others from around the world to end them.

We no longer have to resort to ringing bells of remembrance *after* the tragedies of history. We no longer have to suffer remorse because the lonely resistance efforts of a few failed due to the ignorance and apathy of the many. In that instant, I realized that the communications technology of our time—and the digitally-mediated global culture that it has created—has begun to transform our world in ways that will give powerful new expression to the transcendent reality of human connectedness.

It was then that the idea of *Human Liberty 2.0* was born.

Thanks to digital technologies that have reshaped the way every one of us lives, works, and communicates—technologies that have burst forth at breakneck speed in the last fifteen to twenty years alone—we have suddenly entered a new era of human freedom. Without anyone planning it, a revolution of sorts is unfolding all around us in surprising ways, both at home and in distant corners of the world. Despite the abuses of digital technology, the human race is still collectively finding a path toward a new era of advancing freedom, human rights, and human dignity.

I tried to imagine in my mind what would have happened if the Nazi regime had attempted to liquidate the Warsaw Ghetto in the era of social networking, digital media, and the internet. Instead of stonewalling the Red Cross and the entire free world while covering up their atrocities and genocide, the Nazi regime would have been faced with a flood of tweets, digital videos uploaded online, and a firestorm of public awareness that might have forced the complacent political elites of the world into action much sooner. Of course, the Nazis would have made every attempt to cut off internet access, but we've seen repeatedly in the last few years that there are ways around this—even in the most isolated regions. The power of digital video, satellite imagery, mobile technologies, and more have led to the increasing ability of ordinary people to tell their stories to the world in spite of the heaviest government oppression and censorship imaginable. Those same technologies have also allowed champions for good to sweep in and help in areas where evil may otherwise have continued to thrive.

Indeed, my own journey to the Polish parliament was connected with my personal involvement in precisely such an effort. The long road that had led me to Warsaw that day was part of a larger odyssey of working to develop a human rights education movement on several continents.

Through the vehicle of a number of digital and social media platforms—as well as a growing network of academic centers around the world—the aim of this educational movement is to try to build an international community committed to the good-idea virus of "universal human rights" and the promotion of human dignity in our increasingly global culture. For the first time, in a world historically divided into tribes of geography and tribes of blood, the internet has allowed for the creation of global *tribes of ideas*—groups of people connected in real time across geographic boundary lines by their shared commitment to certain ideals, values, or principles. So, my human rights education work had become focused on trying to create a global idea tribe for universal human rights.

Among other things, this human rights movement-building work had taken me to South Korea, the most digitally advanced nation on Earth, to help promote South Korea's rapid post-Korean War advancement in the realm of human rights as a model for other Asian societies. While working and teaching in South Korea, friends in the Korean National Assembly asked me if I would accompany them to Warsaw for a meeting of European parliamentarians committed to confronting the greatest human rights abuses of our time: the abuses currently taking place in the prison camps of North Korea.

I agreed in part because I knew that no American legislators would be joining their counterparts from South Korea and Eastern Europe at this event. I also made the journey because my exposure to North Korean refugees in South Korea had been a life-changing experience for me. It introduced me to survivors of the North Korean gulag—many of whom have endured unspeakable suffering behind the same electrified barbed wire fences for generations.[2] Finally, I made the journey because my own sense of deep conviction about North Korean human rights had led me to organize a volunteer committee of South Korean marketing professionals in an effort to use digital media to tell the stories of North Korean refugees to a global audience. I was determined to find a digitally-mediated way to replicate in the lives of other people around the world my own transformative experience of hearing the personal stories of men, women, and children who had survived for generations inside a modern-day Auschwitz.

Citizens around the globe rose up to voice their support for the protestors in Egypt during the Arab Spring, thanks to Facebook and Twitter. Similarly, the mainstream media and the US government were finally forced to pay attention to the use of chemical weapons against the citizens of Syria, due to the overwhelming photographic and video evidence shared by ordinary citizens on the Web. In the same way, we need the civilized world to demand an end to this hidden holocaust of our time. North Korea is the most brutal and isolated dictatorship on the planet—in whose prison camps generations languish in torture and darkness. But we must try to support those who are working for freedom amid such darkness. We must hope for the day when new technologies of connectivity will open so many eyes to the death and horror of North Korea that the world will not allow it to continue.

This new era of human liberty is not simply an era of information. *Human Liberty 2.0* describes the beginning of an era of progress—of actually overcoming obstacles, of breaking down barriers, and of saving lives. As you'll see in these pages, the triumph is already under way. The success stories that seem few and far between as we sift through the horror show of the evening news are, in fact, part of one collective movement of the human spirit: A time of technological triumph over barriers to human liberty that have stood for generations.

Our own freedom depends upon our willingness to act on the humanity that unites us all. So the sacrifices of those who fought for freedom in prior generations should inspire us to work together in new ways to resist tyranny and oppression in our time. A new era of human freedom is upon us, and the more we realize it, the more we experience it, the more we share it and celebrate it, the faster the era of *Human Liberty 2.0* will continue to unfold all around us.

CHAPTER 3

HUMAN LIBERTY 2.0: A STORY OF CONVERGENCE

There is a *Human Liberty 2.0* revolution happening across the world to advance freedom, human rights, and human dignity.

The rapid global spread of digital and social media, mobile technologies, and crowd mapping has touched people from every walk of life. Needless to say, not everyone uses these technologies for good. But enough people do that we are seeing a new era of awareness and engagement in the shared enterprise of advancing freedom, resisting oppression, and promoting the dignity of all human beings.

To be sure, there are many disturbing trends in our world. Indeed, the rise of ISIS is a stark reminder that the forces of oppression and evil are still a reality in our time. Moreover, the media is awash with stories that often seem to paint a picture of humanity moving backward. But this book focuses on a global trend that should give us hope for humanity in the Digital Age.

The inspiring, factual stories in Part II of this book—illustrative of countless others that have not been reported or catalogued—are generally not reported as part of the daily news cycle. They are stories of ordinary men and women—some acting individually and some collectively—who are harnessing digital and social media to help promote freedom, human rights, and the dignity of all human beings. Often, they are doing so apart from (or in spite of) those in power. These stories shine a light on an encouraging reality that is quietly unfolding around us—the reality that ordinary people all around the world are finding creative and effective ways to use the power of technology to make the world a better and freer place for us all.

Increasingly, we see stories of individuals who have rallied for causes through Facebook, Twitter, YouTube, and a myriad of digital apps such as WhatsApp and Telegram. At the same time, we are seeing how wireless technologies have helped to bring commerce, food, and supplies to remote areas that weren't being reached before; how crowd mapping is helping to challenge oppressors and put an end to atrocities previously committed in secret.

Human Liberty 2.0 is more than the title of a book. It describes and seeks to catalogue the beginning of a new era in human history—an era that has been unfolding all around us as the internet has changed our world. It seeks to capture trends that are improving human existence in ways that were impossible to achieve only a few short years ago. It's a look at how an expanding catalogue of small stories of technology triumphing over suffering and oppression are not just a few isolated incidents, but a broad trend that offers hope for a greater shared commitment to human dignity in our world.

We are living in exciting times, where solutions that previously seemed elusive are now becoming possible. We are witnessing how the growing connectivity of our world is augmenting the inherent instinct for connectivity in the human spirit—giving us real hope for a more peaceful future. But the future belongs to those who remember the past. So, to fully appreciate our progress thus far—and to make sure it continues—we need to look back and consider how we arrived at this point and what hard-won lessons we can learn from human experience and the struggle for freedom that will help us as we seek to advance together.

Rise of the Rule of Law

There are times in history when new ideas about law create breakthroughs for society. One was the signing of the Magna Carta Libertatum, commonly called Magna Carta, in 1215. The Magna Carta Libertatum, Latin for "The Great Charter of the Liberties," was originally issued by King John of England on June 15, 1215, in an attempt to achieve peace between the king and a group of British nobility who had stood up to their unpopular ruler.[3] In the process, this document became one of the most critical expressions of the concept of fundamental rights and the rule of law.

Among other things, the Magna Carta laid the foundation in Anglo-American law for the revolutionary principle that every person, including royalty, were subject to the rule of law, not above it. This meant that even the king and his government officials could be held accountable for violating the law or depriving others of their fundamental rights. Among its guarantees, the Magna Carta pledged to protect the nobility against illegal incarceration, and to provide access to a swift judicial system and fair trials.

The Magna Carta remains one of the most well-known legal documents in history. Its influence can be seen in a vast number of human rights charters and constitutions, including in the US Constitution. When the United Nations' Universal Declaration of Human Rights was drafted, it also drew upon the freedoms preserved in the Magna Carta. Indeed, given both its origins and international influence, the Universal Declaration has often been called the "Magna Carta for the Digital Age."

The Printing Press Revolution

There are also moments in history when advances in technology transformed the world. One such case was the invention of the Gutenberg printing press in 1439. Borrowing and expanding upon technology that originated in China[4] and that used movable clay script dipped in ink to create text, a German inventor named Johannes Gutenberg sought to improve the clay method of printing text. By using wood (and later, metal) Gutenberg created a mechanical movable-type printing press.

Prior to Gutenberg's invention of the printing press, creating books and other publications was possible, but only one page at a time—a highly laborious undertaking that only the rich could afford. For the same reason, creating hundreds or thousands of books was virtually impossible. This, obviously, was a significant roadblock to acquiring and disseminating new information.

Gutenberg's technology revolutionized printing by enabling the mass production of books for the very first time. The Gutenberg Bible was his first major work. Printed in Latin, the Gutenberg Bible has been celebrated not only for its technical quality but also for its beautiful appearance.

Gutenberg's printing press not only revolutionized book publication, but it also revolutionized mass communication and the diffusion of knowledge, and it laid the foundation for knowledge-based economies and workforces that we still benefit from today. One man's idea for a printing press started the rapid spread of information and learning, first in Europe and then to the rest of the world. Without Gutenberg's invention, the world would be a very different place.

The Concept of Universal Human Rights

World War I was an incredibly bloody affair that resulted in as many as thirty-seven million deaths. The carnage was so overwhelming that it was dubbed "The War to End All Wars." Yet hardly more than a score of years later, the world was plunged yet again into one of the darkest nightmares in all of human history.

World War II ended with more than double the deaths of World War I, and in its wake, mankind was struggling to make sense of what had occurred. By 1948, with the Nuremberg Trials having ended just two years prior, and the shocking travesty of the Holocaust fresh in everyone's mind, there was a palpable determination to defend humanity from future outbreaks of such horrifying oppression. It was in this setting that Eleanor Roosevelt and the framers of the Universal Declaration of Human Rights distilled the most fundamental democratic ideals of justice and freedom into thirty articles that express our common birthright as human beings.[5]

The former First Lady of the United States, who was appointed by President Harry Truman to be part of the US delegation to the United Nations after her husband's death, considered the Universal Declaration of Human Rights to be her greatest achievement. On the ten-year anniversary of the Declaration's adoption, Roosevelt said:

> *Where, after all, do universal human rights begin? In small places, close to home—so close and so small that they cannot be seen on any maps of the world. Yet they are the world of the individual person; the neighborhood he lives in; the school or college he attends; the factory, farm or office where he works. Such are the places where every man, woman and child seeks equal justice, equal opportunity, equal dignity without discrimination. Unless these rights have meaning there, they have little meaning anywhere. Without concerted citizen action to uphold them close to home, we shall look in vain for progress in the larger world.[6]*

The Universal Declaration of Human Rights has become a highly-esteemed legal template for promoting human liberty, having been translated into more languages than any other document in history and having inspired more than eighty international human rights treaties and declarations. But the true significance of the Universal Declaration to the cause of human liberty is only now becoming clear. In our increasingly global and interconnected world, the Universal Declaration is the key to unlocking the profound social potential of the digital revolution because it is the *only* widely-accepted roadmap to a world in which human rights are as universal as the defining communications medium of our time.

The drafters of the Universal Declaration addressed their document not to governments or international agencies, but to all of humanity.[7] They deliberately did so because they believed that human rights enforcement is everyone's business. Moreover, history has shown that human rights are only safe when ordinary men and women see the enforcement of them as their responsibility—not solely the responsibility of those in power— and have the courage to hold those in power accountable.

After all, examples of police brutality and other forms of governmental injustice that rise to the level of human rights violations are best thwarted when ordinary people act on behalf of victims who have no hope of help from the state. Similarly, instances of corporate violations of human rights often cannot be remedied because of government collusion or corruption—so ordinary citizens are critical to confronting such injustices. Even courts and legal bodies that are formally charged with human rights enforcement have been guilty of obscuring, condoning, or even authorizing human rights violations. For example, the United States has seen grave examples of state and federal courts supporting the abuse of human rights—from judicial support for laws condoning slavery and racial segregation to the court-sanctioned internment of an entire ethnic minority, Japanese-Americans, in concentration camps during the Second World War.

At the international level, most people think of the UN as the primary organization responsible for the protection and promotion of human rights. Of course, there is good reason for this view given the unique role that the UN has historically played in the human rights field. Indeed, in this volume, we profile the inspiring stories of charities whose impact can be imputed in significant part to UN support. But there have also been trends and episodes that have called into question the ability of the UN to act as a credible human rights enforcement agency.

At a political level, the human rights machinery of the United Nations is subject to the influence of powerful member states who may not want certain human rights problems to be addressed in regions under their direct control or influence. There's also the problem of corruption seeping into the programs overseen by the UN. The Oil-for-Food Programme in Iraq, established in 1995, is a prime example. It was shut down due to widespread corruption, mismanagement, and unethical conduct after the Coalition Provisional Authority took over in 2003.

In addition, the UN's bureaucracy suffers from the same limitations as other large organizations with respect to high administrative overhead, inefficiency, a lack of transparency, and a relative lack of nimbleness in responding to human rights challenges on the ground. Sometimes the cumulative effect of such factors can be utterly disastrous to the cause of human rights. This was the case in the widely documented UN inaction during the Rwandan genocide in Africa.

In April 1994, amid longstanding tensions caused by tribal animosity, a Central African ethnic group, the Hutus, attempted to exterminate their neighbors, the Tutsis. As a pretext, the Tutsis were being blamed for shooting down an airplane and killing Rwandan President Juvénal Habyarimana in the resulting plane crash.

On April 7, 1994, a Hutu-controlled radio station in the Rwandan capital, Kigali, began calling for the systematic murder and extermination of the Tutsis. Mass killing broke out immediately afterward. One hundred days later, over 800,000 people had been barbarically murdered, mostly by neighbors—former friends—wielding large cleaver-like knives (machetes).[8]

When the commander of the UN peacekeepers in Rwanda, Canadian Lieutenant General Roméo Dallaire, saw the bloodshed breaking out in that spring of 1994, he sought permission to intervene from the UN's New York headquarters, under then-Secretary General Boutros Boutros-Ghali. Gen. Dallaire was denied permission to help the Rwandan people because there was no United Nations peacekeeping resolution with a mandate authorizing him to enforce peace. Gen. Dallaire disobeyed the denial from the United Nations, and in doing so, he and his men were able to save approximately 30,000 lives.[9] But his decision to do this was only even possible because he was there, seeing first-hand what was occurring.

Four years later, former US president Bill Clinton went to Rwanda to apologize for the inaction from the United States and the international community in Rwanda that allowed a mass genocide to take place. President Clinton said, in part:

> *The international community, together with nations in Africa, must bear its share of responsibility for this tragedy, as well. We did not act quickly enough after the killing began. We should not have allowed the refugee camps to become safe havens for the killers. We did not immediately call these crimes by their rightful name: genocide. We cannot change the past. But we can and must do everything in our power to help you build a future without fear, and full of hope. . . .It may seem strange to you here, especially the many of you who lost members of your family, but all over the world there were people like me sitting in offices, day after day after day, who did not fully appreciate the depth and the speed with which you were being engulfed by this unimaginable terror.[10]*

What if Gen. Dallaire and a number of the personnel serving under him in Rwanda had also been using YouTube, Facebook, and Twitter? What if the people of Rwanda had access to social media and were able to share, in real time, the horrors they were witnessing and experiencing with the world? Perhaps the genocide could have been mitigated or even averted in Rwanda, and the history books would have a different ending.

There are moments of humanitarian crisis when there is no time to wait for the United Nations Security Council to vote on a resolution, or to wait for another large international organization or a government to intervene. It is up to individuals to take action.

The good news is more and more people around the world are no longer depending on large, bureaucratic organizations to provide assistance during times of trouble. Individuals have realized that digital and social media are disrupting traditional monopolies and oligarchies of power in fields ranging from journalism to education to disaster relief to commercial entrepreneurship. But what if the same dynamics were to apply in the realm of human rights enforcement?

One of the underlying theories of this book is that the rise of digitally-mediated "tribes of ideas" has created a historically-unprecedented opportunity for an expansion of citizen engagement in the human rights enterprise. From one perspective, this may sound quixotic, given the many forces in our world that pose a threat to freedom and human dignity. But one can already see in the small sample of inspiring stories catalogued in this book a myriad of individuals and groups—from many different parts of our world—all working to advance fundamental rights through digital and social media. From this perspective, it seems much more plausible to dream that the Universal Declaration of Human Rights was a legal birth certificate for one of the greatest ideas in human history—the vision of universal rights for all—that was awaiting the advent of the Digital Age to become a meaningful social and cultural reality.

The Convergence of Law and Technology

Today, we are witnessing the extraordinary convergence of two break-throughs *at the same time*: the advancement of *universal rights* in the hands of a digital generation using the *World Wide Web*. This is a convergence with vast potential to unleash human creativity and compassion. But the interconnectedness of the Digital Age also carries responsibilities for each of us.

Technology is morally neutral. It can be used for good or evil. At a certain dosage, drugs alleviate pain and cure illness. At another dosage, the same drugs can cause addiction or death. The same applies to digital media and computer technology. The benefits are enormous and far-reaching...except when digital technology is misused for activities such as child pornography, cybercrime, or worse. Indeed, as we shall see in this book, powerful forces in our world are working to harness all the tools of digital media for evil. Terrorist movements employ digital media to recruit and to spread violent propaganda in support of slavery and genocide. Repressive governments use digital media to violate privacy, censor speech, crush artistic freedom, oppress their critics, and deny citizens their fundamental rights. But then this is nothing new, and frankly, as students of history know, it ought to be anticipated. The key in every age and every revolution, though, is to take those same powerful technological tools and use them for good rather than evil. The question is how should we respond?

This book was written to inspire future generations with the stories of courageous men and women around the world and how they have answered the call. Our task now is to use the tools of the Digital Age to tell these stories and teach the principles of the Universal Declaration to as broad an audience as possible—to spread the good-idea virus and build a global idea tribe around the concept of universal human rights and the universality of human dignity as the birthright of every human being—and in so doing, motivate others to follow in their footsteps.

CHAPTER 4

NETIZENS RISING: DIGITAL DAVIDS VERSUS GOLIATHS

Remember the story of a young Jewish boy named David who ran into battle armed with nothing more than a leather strap and a few rocks? Driven by a sense of justice, he had the courage to challenge a power that had terrified an entire army of older soldiers stronger and more proficient in battle than he was. With a single slingshot, David defeated the formerly invincible giant, Goliath, and freed his people oppressed by the Philistines. Even if you regard the story as mythical, it is a reminder that the forces of violence and oppression can sometimes be toppled by the courage of those who are willing to fight against the odds—even if they are younger than those who have made their peace with injustice. This is especially true when we work together in the many potent ways that the internet has made possible in our time.

At its simplest, "Web 2.0" is a term often used to describe how the internet has gone far beyond a platform for passive connection between distant audiences. Similarly, we are now witnessing the expanding power of human connection to advance universal rights. The ability to topple Goliaths of every description is now in the hands of millions of "Digital Davids." All around the world, these internet citizens—"netizens"—are using the Web to:

- Expose the lies of tyrants;

- Break dictatorial information monopolies;

- Free democratic creativity;

- Publicize the illegitimate actions of their oppressors;

- Defend the dignity of all people as our common human birthright.

We live in an era when the internet—backed by a rising global conscience with respect to universal human rights—is networking these Digital Davids into a collective slingshot for the promotion of human liberty. This same revolutionary convergence is also creating communities of virtually-connected Good Samaritans who are reaching across the barriers of geography and culture to help people utterly unlike themselves around the world.

Of course, we are also seeing many national governments desperately trying to control this medium of communication to invade privacy and control people's lives. The same could be said of some powerful companies motivated by profit. But even in these cases, a rising generation of Digital Davids has seen some success against some of the biggest Goliaths of our age.

Consider the recent examples of the role that digital media has played in Egypt and China—in spite of the powerful forces of oppression operating in both countries. A frustrated Egyptian ruler, in January 2011, flipped the switch to take the country off the internet. It didn't work out too well for him.[11] The genie of aspiration for human liberty was already out of the bottle and had gathered a crowd, thanks to the internet.

China has devoted vast resources in an effort to control and censor its netizens. The communist government bought the best technology from around the world and added new censorship technologies of its own. Yet, as we shall see later in this book, Chinese netizens are still getting around the "Great Firewall of China." Indeed, millions of these Chinese Digital Davids are going to the Web to communicate their grievances against corruption and other abuses endemic in the communist party monopoly on power such that the greatest governmental Goliath in the world cannot completely silence them all.

Around the globe, in the small and large places of human flourishing, we are living in the midst of an unprecedented era of transformation for human liberty. This extraordinary period has only just begun. We are still in the early stages of the organic convergence of the greatest breakthrough for human rights in history with the greatest global communications breakthrough that the world has ever seen.

Thanks to ordinary digital humanitarians working in their homes, internet cafes, and university computer labs, a new frontier in the fight for human liberty has been established. Human beings are employing digital and social media to accelerate human liberty in ways that were previously impossible—and sometimes on a global scale. These promising breakthroughs for human liberty provide a growing body of evidence that the global convergence of universal rights and the World Wide Web may be inevitable. For the sake of future generations, let us all hope and work to that end.

It is our hope that the rise of a generation of digital natives raised on the Web—who naturally tend to think more globally than earlier generations—will create increasing opportunities for the sort of stories that are catalogued in this book; stories of ordinary citizens who rise to the challenge of the vision of the Universal Declaration to make human rights the work of the entire human race. In fact, we hope that reading this book will make you want to join in the revolution that we call *Human Liberty 2.0*.

11

DIGITAL HUMANITARIANS: THE UNSUNG HEROES OF *HUMAN LIBERTY 2.0*

CHAPTER 5

THE COMPASSION OF CROWDS

Throughout history, crowds have generally not been associated with compassion. On the contrary, they are often associated with the worst instincts in human nature. So, it is all the more remarkable to be living in an era when digitally-mediated crowds can be meaningful agents of compassion in times of crisis.

In December 2007, when ethnic violence and bloodshed ripped through the streets of Kenya over vote-rigging and disputed election results between Raila Odinga's Orange Democratic Movement (ODM) and incumbent president Mwai Kibaki's Party of National Unity (PNU), the government tried to downplay the violence in the media. Meanwhile, *The New York Times* reported, "In several cities across Kenya, witnesses said, gangs went house to house, dragging out people of certain tribes and clubbing them to death."[12]

In some places there were virtual blackouts of information. People who desperately needed help could not get any.

The horrific post-election violence, a war between the Kikuyus and Luo tribes that continued throughout Kenya until February the following year, left more than 1,200 people dead and displaced approximately half a million individuals who were forced to flee for their lives.

At one point, Alfred Mutua, the Kenyan government spokesperson, charged that "Raila Odinga's supporters" were "engaged in ethnic cleansing" and attacked with "military precision." Machete-wielding bandits were murdering people based on their ethnicity.[13] In one case, women and children who sought refuge in a church were burned alive.

How could anyone provide help where it was needed and stop the violence without accurate, actionable information? A group of tech-savvy social entrepreneurs in the capital, Nairobi, rose to the challenge and filled the void that the government and the international community could not or would not. Juliana Rotich, Ory Okolloh, David Kobia, and Erik Hersman created and co-founded what became Ushahidi.[14]

"Ushahidi" is Swahili for "testimony" or "witness." Using open-source software, they created a website with an interactive map of Kenya. Using information collected from social media, as well as mainstream and official reports, the map was constantly being updated with the latest information about the violence that was taking place in the country.

The concept behind Ushahidi is to use information collected from social media platforms including Twitter, Facebook, YouTube videos, Flickr, text messages, blog posts, smart phone apps, and Skype, and integrate it all in one map, providing crisis reporting through "crowd mapping."

Crowd mapping enabled individuals who wanted to help people in Kenya to pitch in from wherever they were—digital Good Samaritans made up of volunteers, journalists, citizens, witnesses in Kenya, and other people outside of Kenya. All of the above were involved in capturing events as they were unfolding and updating information on the map.

As a result, resources and aid could be moved to where it was most needed.

Ushahidi's map provided a free platform where people could circumvent the Kenyan government and allow the unfettered, free flow of information.

Ushahidi also filled another important void. It is impossible for journalists to be everywhere and report all human rights abuses as they occur. Ushahidi became a unique collaboration tool for citizen journalists to use during a crisis. In this way, it gave voice to the voiceless. It empowered average individuals with access to the internet to inform the world on what they were witnessing first hand and in some cases, in real time. Since the post-election violence in Kenya, Ushahidi's crowd-source mapping has expanded to include people from all over the world. It has also been used in an increasingly wide array of contexts. For example, the platform has been used to generate maps documenting corruption, environmental mapping, and even election fraud.

Ushahidi-Haiti

On January 10, 2010, a catastrophic 7.0 magnitude earthquake rocked Haiti. In its wake, more than 230,000 people were killed and approximately 1.5 million were left homeless and displaced. Chaos, confusion, and death ensued.[15]

Within a couple of hours of the earthquake, one particularly talented digital Good Samaritan in Boston, Patrick Meier, wanted to do something to assist the Haitian people in their distress. He created an Ushahidi-Haiti map. With the help of some students from Tufts University, the crowd-sourced crisis reporting effort for Haiti began.

The first social media sources for the Ushahidi-Haiti map were found on Twitter from people who were tweeting live.[16] In some cases, individuals who were trapped under rubble disclosed their location. As a result, rescue teams were notified and dispatched to rescue them.

Day after day, more and more volunteers showed up, adding to Haiti's crisis-mapping capabilities. Soon there were students in London, Toronto, Geneva, and Washington who were drawing information from social media, news reports, and official reports and mapping it all. Thousands of Haitian-American volunteers, who spoke Creole, volunteered online to support the effort. Within minutes, texts from survivors in Haiti who spoke Creole, and other information coming from various social media sources, were all translated.

The Ushahidi-Haiti map rarely looked the same. Like the Ushahidi map of Kenya, it, too, was a *living* map that kept changing with the latest updated information—and it was a map that was literally giving life to survivors struggling in the rubble.

By providing volunteers in other parts of the world with access to Ushahidi's free platform and tools, life-saving information was made available to first responders, relief organizations, and others in the crisis zone, who were then empowered to help where the needs were most dire.

Thanks to the power of digital media, it was not a large, well-funded government agency or the United Nations who created this map of Haiti, full of critical information on where to direct vital resources and aid. It was individuals, digital Good Samaritans like Meier coming together from all over the world, who created the lifesaving Ushahidi-Haiti map. In short, Ushahidi-Haiti was far more effective than what the United Nations and other international relief agencies were doing on their own.

About a week after the earthquake, the head of the Federal Emergency Management Agency (FEMA) acknowledged that the Ushahidi-Haiti map was the most detailed and comprehensive map he'd ever seen.

In an email, a US Marine who worked as part of a rescue effort in Haiti wrote, "I cannot overemphasize to you what the work of the Ushahidi-Haiti has provided. It is saving lives every day.... You are making the biggest difference of anything I have seen out there in the open source world."[17]

Due to the amazing life-saving impact of Ushahidi-Haiti and Ushahidi-Kenya, Patrick Meier has become an internationally-recognized expert and consultant on the innovative use of technology for humanitarian purposes. Among his many projects, Meier went on to create crisismappers.net.[18]

Crisis Mappers Net is unique in that it is not a typical organization but rather a network—a network of people sharing information and collectively crowd-mapping to enable rapid responses to humanitarian crises around the world.

Crisis Mappers Net includes over 9,300 members in over 160 countries, who are affiliated with over 3,000 different institutions, including universities, United Nations agencies, first responders, dozens of leading technology companies, and local disaster response and recovery organizations.[19]

Clearly, Meier's vision for using digital media to save and improve human lives has become a burgeoning reality in our time. His example is proof that individuals can make a difference in helping other human beings with the powerful digital tools available in the era of *Human Liberty 2.0*. Ushahidi illustrates the power of ordinary people to use the internet to be digital Good Samaritans—across boundaries of geography and culture—in ways never before possible in human history.

CHAPTER 6

THE PEOPLE ARE THE PRESS

The First Amendment of the US Constitution states: "Congress shall make no law respecting an establishment of religion, or prohibiting the free exercise thereof; or abridging the freedom of speech, or of the press; or the right of the people peaceably to assemble, and to petition the Government for a redress of grievances."

The international version of the free speech provisions of the First Amendment is Article 19 of the Universal Declaration: "Everyone has the right to freedom of opinion and expression; this right includes freedom to hold opinions without interference and to seek, receive and impart information and ideas through any media and regardless of frontiers."

Significantly, whereas "freedom of the press" has historically been applied to traditional news media (reporters and editors for newspapers, television, and so on) the digital media revolution is rapidly expanding the meaning of the pre-digital term "press" to include everyone—including bloggers and citizens posting digital videos online. Indeed, due to this blurring of the lines between professional and citizen journalists and commentators, many repressive regimes around the world are targeting and punishing citizens for their online activities with the same harshness previously reserved for campaigns to silence traditional media outlets deemed to be hostile or critical of those in power.

As a result of these trends, many people in the world today live under conditions where freedom of speech and the press are systematically denied—with authoritarian societies displaying an increasing level of animosity to these freedoms, as digital and social media provide increasingly more powerful tools to citizen journalists. In some societies, oppressive regimes even claim that freedom of speech and freedom of the press represent violations of important cultural and religious traditions. For example, some Communist regimes claim that these freedoms are not needed in a harmonious socialist society where the interests of the people and the government are allegedly the same. Similarly, some Islamic regimes claim that these freedoms are tantamount to an attack upon the Islamic religious faith and its values. This line of argument is especially prevalent in the developing world, where governments will sometimes deceptively seek to pit other basic human needs against fundamental human rights. Given that so many governments will go to such great lengths to suppress the power of people to communicate and share information, we need to ask the obvious question: *Why are freedom of speech and the press so important?*

Without freedom of speech and a free press, we are in the dark about critical issues—including the violation of human rights—that affect us, our families, and large numbers of other people. Despotic regimes ruling with an iron fist and oppressing their citizens, for example, would never be exposed or face any accountability. Corrupt politicians engaged in illegal activities for their personal gain would persist without public exposure. Child laborers would multiply, women would be treated like second class citizens, and girls would continue to be denied the right to receive an education. Shining a light on such problems has, at times, actually stopped bloodshed, helped save people in peril, and exposed basic human right abuses.

In the West we often take our freedom of speech and the freedom of the press for granted, but for citizens, journalists, and netizens in other parts of the world, free speech and the free flow of information is not a right they enjoy.

Did you know that authoritarian regimes around the world treat online critics as enemies of the state on par with terrorists? These leaders predictably borrow from each other's playbooks in a recurring theme: (1) attack the press; (2) label and defame individuals who dare to criticize their policies—often labeling them as foreign agents; and (3) incarcerate or eliminate all such opposing voices as a threat to society.

In the eyes of oppressive governments, like Vietnam, Saudi Arabia, Turkey, Iran, Russia, North Korea, and many other nations whose leaders are determined to control their citizens, so-called "terrorists" can be individuals who have been risking their lives and safety simply in the defense of the free flow of information.

Reporters Without Borders, the largest press freedom organization in the world, has been on the front lines protecting freedom of speech, journalists' safety, and fighting censorship since it was founded in France in 1985. Made up of a network of 150 correspondents in 130 countries, Reporters Without Borders monitors, investigates, and draws attention to attacks on the freedom of expression and of information wherever they may occur and makes legal recommendations to reform media laws.[20] In addition, Reporters Without Borders has been able to provide lifesaving assistance to journalists and netizens who are operating in unstable environments and are in danger, including disaster areas and war zones.

One of Reporters Without Borders's online tracker tools is their "Press Freedom Barometer." It identifies and records the last known location of all journalists and media workers in countries who have been killed or imprisoned that it could verify. Alarmingly, with the arrival and swift growth of social media, Reporters Without Borders needed to add a new category to their Press Freedom Barometer.[21] Tragically, it now includes tracking netizens and citizen journalists who have been killed, are facing persecution, or are in prison and need help.

In the event of persecution or unlawful imprisonment, Reporters Without Borders is quick to establish online petitions to generate pressure on the government authorities involved to release the detainee(s). Raif Badawi, a thirty-five-year-old citizen-journalist and website creator in

Saudi Arabia, is one of the netizens they are trying to free—and also spare from being brutally lashed 1,000 times in public. In September 2014, Badawi was sentenced to ten years in a Saudi Arabian prison because he "publicly questioned the way the Saudi Society is evolving and its respect for fundamental freedoms, thereby prompting a debate about political, religious and social issues."[22]

No longer safe in their homeland of Saudi Arabia, his wife, Ensaf Haidar, with their three young children, fled to Canada, where they were granted asylum. A nonprofit organization, "The Raif Badawi Foundation for Freedom," was established and a "Free Raif Badawi" Facebook page was created to help keep the pressure on the Saudi government for Badawi's release and to keep the public informed of the latest developments.[23] Supported by many international human rights groups, and with the assistance from different leaders in the international community, the online and offline campaign to free Badawi continues.

In June 2018, the Ukrainian news agency *Ukrinform's* Paris correspondent, Roman Sushchenko, was sentenced to twelve years in a "high security prison camp" by a Moscow court, allegedly for espionage, a charge Sushchenko denies. According to *Ukrinform,* Sushchendo was arrested while on vacation visiting family in Russia. *Ukrinform* praised Sushchenko as "a journalist with many years of impeccable professional reputation." The undisclosed evidence against Sushchenko remains highly suspect, as the proceedings were conducted in secret and the indictment remains classified.[24]

Since the US invasion of Iraq and the overthrow of its former dictator, Saddam Hussein, over 207 journalists have been killed in Iraq, but currently, the most dangerous country for journalists to operate in is Syria. Since civil war broke out in March 2011, over 168 news providers have been killed, including fourteen foreign journalists. At least nineteen Syrian journalists have been detained by the terror group ISIS and thirty by Syrian president Bashar al-Assad's regime.

China, Vietnam, Eritrea, Syria, Iran, Ethiopia, and Uzbekistan hold the dubious distinction for imprisoning the largest number of news providers. Worldwide in 2015, there were 167 journalists and media assistants imprisoned and 184 netizens locked up. As of December 2017, the disturbing trend rose to 202 professional journalists, 107 netizens, and seventeen media workers detained.

As Delphine Halgand-Mishra, the former North American Director of Reporters Without Borders, explains, "We've seen a change with the increase of social media. Bloggers, a citizen passing information on Facebook or Twitter can be targeted, arrested, or censored as much as traditional journalists were in the past. This shows the importance and the reach of social media."

In repressive societies, to an increasing degree, social media is being treated like traditional media—with the result that anyone's social media activity can put them in danger. In the Middle East you can be arrested for tweets. In Mexico, a blogger was murdered for posting negative statements about the drug cartels on Facebook. When his body was found there was a note pinned to his chest warning others, "This is because of what you posted on Facebook," the note said.

China, Vietnam, and North Korea have increased their internet controls and clamped down on online activity within their borders—attempts to censor the internet and stifle free speech never take a break.

According to a Reporters Without Borders's annual report, China's Great Firewall, as its censorship system is known, is getting "higher." North Korea has put into place "special squads" to enforce its "wall of silence." Vietnam's new decree to suppress online dissent is "even tougher" than their previous internet laws. Reporters Without Borders goes on to explain how "Officials have also expanded their use of a 'nuisance' approach of targeting online dissidents with in-person monitoring, to the point where being followed in the street and other forms of surveillance 'have become a part of daily life' for Vietnamese bloggers."

As Halgand-Mishra of Reporters Without Borders elaborated, "Oppressive governments try to control information. In Thailand, for instance, citizens have also been arrested and sentenced to prison for what they have written on Facebook. In China, where nearly one-fifth of the world's population lives, you cannot access Facebook or Twitter at all. It is banned. To access the non-censored internet a person has to use a VPN—a Virtual Private Network." As of March 31, 2018, VPNs are also banned in China, although they are still widely available.

These severe restrictions clearly demonstrate that oppressive regimes recognize the power of digital and social media and the threat it poses to their grip on power, especially in an era when the people increasingly *are* the press. And in such circumstances, people like Raif Badawi and groups like Reporters Without Borders are heroes, advocating for everyone's basic rights when they promote freedom of the press and the free flow of information. They are on the frontlines in humanity's struggle to spread the good idea virus of universal rights through digital and social media.

CHAPTER 7

THE LIFEBLOOD OF
HUMAN LIBERTY 2.0

Internet censorship is not an isolated problem in a small number of countries—it is a widespread challenge to the digital and social media that are the lifeblood of *Human Liberty 2.0*. Wherever internet censorship prevails, evil and oppression are given more room to flourish. Censorship is all the more pernicious when it is touted as an alleged ideological or religious virtue. For example, some Islamic nations punish any public or private speech considered critical of official religious dogma or polices with imprisonment, torture, and even death.

In the Islamic Republic of Iran, Canadian-Iranian Hossein Derakhshan was sentenced in 2010, by an Iranian court, to serve nineteen years in prison. His crime? According to the Iranian website *Mashreghnews*, Derakhshan was convicted by Iran's Revolutionary Court of "cooperating with hostile states," "propaganda in favor of counter-revolutionary groups," and "insults to the holy sanctities" for his blogging online.[25]

Derakhshan, who has done most of his blogging from outside Iran, led the Iranian blogging revolution that paved the way for what became known as the Green Movement.

During the highly passionate and violently disputed June 12, 2009, presidential elections between then-sitting president Mahmoud Ahmadinejad and opposition candidates Mir-Hossein Mousavi and Mehdi

Karroubi, the public was told that President Ahmadinejad had officially been reelected in a landslide vote. Furthermore, they were told the election turnout was high—another official claim designed to legitimize his regime's hold on power. But a large percentage of Iranians did not trust the "official" election results and, in their anger and disbelief, ignited what became the Green Movement.[26]

Scores of men and women of all ages peacefully poured onto the streets in protest. "Where is my vote?" became their simple slogan. They collectively became a dissenting grassroots movement known as the "Green Movement" demanding basic human rights and fair elections from their leadership.

The Green Movement in Iran is also known as the Twitter Revolution because Twitter and other social media platforms, including YouTube, pulled back the curtain for the rest of the world and exposed what was happening in the otherwise secretive nation. The peaceful protests quickly turned violent as the authoritarian government brutally suppressed the revolution and its own citizens. Numerous protesters went missing, were jailed, or were killed.[27] This included a young woman named Neda Agha-Soltan, a young philosophy student who was shot in the chest by police in the streets of Tehran. Many other protestors died on the same day as victims of government violence against the Iranian people, their names known only to their friends and family. But Neda Agha-Soltan's death drew worldwide attention to the brutality of the Iranian regime when a video of her death was uploaded to YouTube. Millions of people around the world watched as this beautiful young girl slowly bled to death in the street—gazing up at the camera—while bystanders frantically tried to save her life.

In the past several years, the Iranian theocratic dictatorship has brought vaguely worded charges against hundreds of online dissenters, landing many of them in prison. In June 2015, for example, Iran's judicial system spokesman, Gholam-Hossein Mohseni-Eje´i, announced the arrests of "several individuals" for social network activity vaguely described as "actions against national security."

The victims of Iran's Revolutionary Guard roundup include Mahmud Moussavifar and Shayan AkbarPour, two internet activists who ran the Rahian Facebook page and a blog called Rahi, which can no longer be accessed.[28]

Journalist, passionate human rights advocate, and former deputy of the "Defenders of Human Rights Center in Iran," Narges Mohammadi, had been arrested one month earlier, in May 2015. Mohammadi was sentenced to five years for the charge of "meeting and plotting against the Islamic Republic," one year for "anti-government propaganda," and ten years for her efforts to end the death penalty in Iran.[29]

In 2017 she wrote a heartbreaking open letter from prison, pleading to be released. In part, it read, "I do not have a real and clear image of my twins, anymore." Since she was imprisoned, her young twins have been living in Paris with her husband in exile.[30] Mohammadi remains in prison in Iran today.

This year Reporters Without Borders ranked Iran 164 out of 180 countries in their 2018 World Press Freedom index, making it among one of the worst offending countries. In Iran, where criticizing the supreme leader or his regime's policies often results in long and prison sentences, human rights abuses continue unabated.

There is no freedom of speech in Iran. All public speech remains heavily censored and restricted, both offline and online. As a result, journalists find themselves self-censoring simply as a matter of self-preservation.[31]

Among the social media responses calling for the world to stand with the people of Iran is a global network of musicians from countries including Iran, Libya, Egypt, United States, South Africa, and Sweden, who formed a group called United for Iran, which collaborated with artists and musicians to create an album called *Azadi: Songs of Freedom for Iran.*[32]

This global collaboration of artists, many of whom have had direct experiences with repression themselves, wrote "Songs of Freedom for Iran" with united4iran.org. By using the power of several social media tools, including Twitter, Facebook, and YouTube, the album spread the freedom message using a collection of inspirational songs to give voice to the Iranian people and their struggle. The song titles speak for themselves, including "Revolution of the Mind," "Die for My People," and "Freedom Glory Be Our Name."[33]

Today, Iranians are still seeking democracy and basic human rights from their oppressive government, but now the world is watching. Groups like United for Iran continue their efforts on behalf of the Iranian people.

Advancing human rights is not easy. It can be outright dangerous and result in sacrifices that most people in the West cannot fully fathom or imagine. Given the struggle and sacrifice required in places such as Iran, we would do well to remember one of Mahatma Gandhi's notable insights: "Satisfaction lies in the effort, not in the attainment. Full effort is full victory."

Gandhi, a courageous leader and Indian activist for democracy, changed the world when he peacefully protested British rule in India by advocating change through nonviolent disobedience. But he had no guarantee of success when he took on the most powerful empire in the world.

In the spirit of this wise admonition, we should do what we can to raise awareness and challenge regimes that suppress dissent, including attacks on freedom of speech. Today we have the internet to make a difference and shine a bright light on the offenders. We should make maximum use of these tools while we have them since otherwise they can be lost. Freedom of speech, in all its forms, must be protected as the lifeblood of *Human Liberty 2.0.*

CHAPTER 8

DRIVING CHANGE IN A HUMAN RIGHTS DESERT

In spite of efforts to censor the internet and stifle free speech in countries all over the world, part of the story of *Human Liberty 2.0* is the remarkable, inspirational stories of how courageous social media pioneers are advancing democracy and calling attention to the plight of people in some of the most oppressive countries.

As Reporters Without Borders's Delphine Halgand-Mishra explained in an interview for this book, "One example is the movement that was started by one Saudi woman who posted a video of herself driving in Saudi Arabia, where, until this past summer, women were forbidden to drive. She was arrested, but because of the reaction, in large part from social media, she was released days later. As a result of her actions, more Saudi women began posting themselves driving on YouTube and were not arrested. Now the authorities are slowly beginning to ease up on the restrictions for women. That is a huge step forward for all women in Saudi Arabia, and it's a peaceful and democratic way to affect positive change."

During a TED talk, Manal al-Sharif, the brave Saudi woman who was put in jail for daring to drive a car in Saudi Arabia, uploading a video of it on YouTube, and defying the status quo, gave a moving account of her unlikely journey to becoming an internationally-celebrated activist and role model for women.[34]

TED, a conference where people gather for short talks that are later broadcast on the internet, began in 1984. It's a nonprofit organization "devoted to spreading ideas…and today covers almost all topics—from science to business to global issues."

Al-Sharif began her TED talk like this: "Allow me to ask this question. All over the world people fight for their freedom—fight for their rights. Some battle oppressive governments, others oppressive society. Which battle do you think is harder?"[35]

Her question is an important one that does not have an easy answer. But it should encourage us to ponder the multidimensional challenges that such human rights pioneers face.

Let's look at her experience to shed some light on daunting realities of her struggle.

It was May 2011 and al-Sharif was frustrated because she was having trouble arranging rides and getting around. In Saudi Arabia there is no public transportation. Since women in Saudi Arabia have the legal status of minor children, she needs a man—a so-called "male guardian"—to drive her where she needs to go.

Her frustration grew. Al-Sharif had a car and an international driver's license that she could use everywhere else around the world except in her own country.

She began to investigate why women in Saudi Arabia are not allowed to drive. She soon learned that there were no actual laws on the books making it illegal. Denying a woman the right to drive was a man-made custom found in "fatwas," or religious decrees from Saudi Muslim clerics.

Since it was not illegal for Saudi women to drive, why shouldn't they drive? Al-Sharif decided to start the Women2Drive campaign, calling on others to join her on Facebook.

As Al-Sharif recounted in her book, *Daring to Drive: A Saudi Woman's Awakening*:

I'd learned the proper rules of driving when I was living in the U.S.—I got a New Hampshire and then a Massachusetts driver's license. But in Saudi Arabia, I never got behind the wheel. Saudi women rely

on drivers to ferry them from place to place. We are at their mercy.
Almost every woman I know has been harassed by a driver. They make
comments about our appearance; they demand more money; they
touch us inappropriately. Some women have been attacked. I've had
drivers make all sorts of inappropriate comments and tape my calls
when I've used my cell phone, thinking maybe they could blackmail or
extort me.[36]

As she got behind the wheel in Saudi Arabia she was excited but terrified at the same time. Shortly after uploading a video of her driving on YouTube, she was amazed by the thunderous response. Her video views rapidly skyrocketed into the hundreds of thousands, creating a viral phenomenon.[37] She also started receiving death threats. To the outside world, she quickly became a hero, but to many in her own country, she was a villain.

The government had her arrested and thrown in jail. She was considered a threat to the social order and therefore to the legitimacy of the government itself. And not just her. Her brother was also arrested—twice—just for giving her his car keys. Once released, he left his job as a geologist and, with his wife and their two-year-old son, fled the country.

Outside the prison the country seemed to be in a frenzy. Protests both for and against the driving ban began to break out. Al-Sharif faced an orchestrated social backlash. She became the focus of a highly-organized defamation campaign, where false statements about her were widely publicized in an attempt to harm her reputation, credibility, and standing in the conservative Saudi society.

Members of her immediate family attending Friday services at their local mosque with thousands of other worshippers, many of whom were extended family and friends, had to sit through an imam's sermon in which he condemned women drivers like her, calling them prostitutes. And he wasn't the only one. Other Saudi clerics began an ugly campaign against al-Sharif, calling for her to be flogged in public simply for driving a car.[38] In Saudi Arabia, such violent, medieval public punishment—along with even more barbaric practices such as stoning—are still used against perceived enemies of the social order even today.

In the media of the free world, she was being described as the Saudi Rosa Parks,[39] but at home she was called every degrading name imaginable—not just a prostitute, but a traitor and a blasphemer, too. This was the social punishment for daring to challenge the long-held Saudi social rules. One of the Saudi headlines in a publication called *Alwatan* wrote that Manal al-Sharif faced charges of "disturbing public order" for inciting women to drive. In this respect, the charges against her echoed the accusations leveled against Dr. Martin Luther King Jr. and his followers for allegedly "inciting violence" by daring to challenge racial apartheid in the American South.[40] Another Saudi publication falsely claimed she had broken down and confessed that "foreign forces incited" her to do this. She was widely condemned for "corrupting society."

What al-Sharif did simply by driving was considered outrageous to the ultra-conservative leadership of Saudi Arabia. After all, it speaks volumes that Saudi Arabia is one of only three nations in 1948 to have abstained from approving the Universal Declaration of Human Rights.

From the founding of Saudi Arabia to the present day, women still do not enjoy anything remotely resembling the freedoms that Saudi men take for granted. The law is a teacher, and when a law systematically sends a negative message about the abilities or rights of a given group of people, it provides legal support for a much wider culture of discrimination, oppression, and even violence in a society. In this context, it's much easier to understand why the Saudi driving ban was such a big deal. It was part of a larger and systematic Saudi denial of legal equality and freedom for women not unlike the movement for suffrage in America, which was part of a bigger struggle for social and political equality for women in the United States.

Manal al-Sharif, a woman who faced both an oppressive society and government at the same time, stated, "I'm a proud Saudi woman who loves my country, and because I love my country, I am doing this. I believe a society will not be free until women of that society are free."

When al-Sharif was released from jail after nine days, she first took a shower and then she checked her Twitter and Facebook accounts. She was amazed to see the response on social media supporting her.

Al-Sharif's courageous act in defiance of an oppressive Saudi Arabian regime took the battle for women's rights and the right to drive in Saudi Arabia to the world stage. Prior to her YouTube video, this long-standing battle had been waged by human rights activists largely unnoticed. Al-Sharif's YouTube video started the important, necessary, and long overdue conversation to lift the ban on women driving.

Meaningful and measurable progress takes time and persistence. It can be messy and frightening and include unfathomable sacrifices. This has been true throughout history, as the lives of civil right leaders like Mahatma Gandhi and Dr. King clearly demonstrate. Both men faced governmental and societal oppression. They were jailed, subjected to threats, assaults, and eventually death. But by virtue of their power and appeal, over time they have triumphed.

Similarly, al-Sharif's life was forever changed the day she dared to drive. She never set out to be an activist, and would ultimately be banned from Saudi Arabia. Although she now lives in Australia, she maintains the hope of being able to return to her home one day and drive—the way all other women in Saudi Arabia now can, thanks in large part to the Women-2Drive campaign that was started by one very courageous Digital David.

Despite fear of punishment, including imprisonment, one hundred women drove the day al-Sharif was released from prison. None of them was arrested. Together they broke the oppressive social taboo, and as a result, Saudi Arabia is finally heading down the road (so to speak) toward advancing women's freedom.

The Power of Satire and Digital Video

In addition to spurring other women to drive and moving human rights forward in Saudi Arabia, al-Sharif inspired others around the world who took to the internet to raise awareness of other human rights abuses for women in Saudi Arabia.

In one case, an artist and social activist who calls himself Hisham Fageeh used musical satire to mock the oppressors while making an important social point about women's equality. Satire can be a powerful tool to undermine the legitimacy of a policy or practice, particularly when disseminated widely. So, when Fageeh's parody of the famous Bob Marley song, "No Woman, No Cry," went viral on YouTube, it, too, made a significant impact on the thinking of Saudis viewers.

To give satirical voice to the struggle of Saudi women, he renamed Marley's song, "No Woman, No Drive,"[41] and using masterful digital editing techniques, this artist and activist created an a cappella choir— composed of multiple digital versions of himself—dressed in traditional Saudi male garb. Together, this chorus of one sang:

Say I remember when you used to sit
In the family car, but backseat
Ova-ovaries all safe and well
So you can make lots and lots of babies
Good friends we had and good friends we lost
On the highway
In this bright future you can't forget your past
So put your car key away
Hey, little sister, don't touch that wheel
No woman, no drive!

His brilliantly creative derision of Saudi Arabia's man-made rules spoke volumes. It resonated with millions of viewers. It also illustrates how humor and satire are powerful intellectual weapons that can strip away fear, challenge assumptions, and undermine oppression. Employing the tools of digital and social media, virtually anyone can become a Digital David and raise awareness of human rights issues in our time.

Of course, the hard work of meaningful social change often requires great courage and sacrifice. But thoughtful, well-targeted satire can also play a powerful role in discrediting and undermining the bankrupt policies and ideologies of those in power.

More Work Still to Do

In September 2017, more than six years after Manal al-Sharif posted online the video of herself driving, Saudi leadership announced by a royal decree the driving ban would be lifted on June 24, 2018. As the *Saudi Press Agency* reported, "The royal decree will implement the provisions of traffic regulations, including the issuance of driving licenses for men and women alike."

While the decree sounded good and sincere, the world was shocked when, just weeks before the ban was due to be lifted, Saudi authorities detained at least seven women for driving. Some activists feared the changes would be superficial and not translate to meaningful freedom on the ground.

But then, as the clock passed midnight on June 24, 2018, women in Saudi Arabia who were able to get licenses took to the streets in major cities like Riyadh and Jeddah and started to drive. It was beautiful—an historic moment.

"I feel free like a bird!" one Saudi woman exclaimed while driving. Others cheered in delight; some cried, overwhelmed with joy. Carefully, in what some people say were staged events to show the Saudi regime in the best possible light, police officers, who twenty-four hours earlier would have arrested these women who were driving, instead handed out flowers to them.[42]

Saudi billionaire Prince Alwaleed bin Talal, an early purported advocate of women driving, released a video of his daughter driving shortly after midnight on June 24. "Saudi Arabia has just entered the 21st century," he told his granddaughters in the back seat.[43]

But such voices are only whitewashing the underlying problem regarding the oppression that Saudi women will still face as human beings with the legal status of minor children who are otherwise totally dependent upon men.

On one hand the regime will allow Saudi women to be able to drive to a doctor—only to be denied healthcare unless they have secured a male guardian's permission. The same applies for driving to the bank, their workplace, or the airport. All such facilities remain solely the province of men—and women are only allowed to access them with male permission. So, the deep inequality at the heart of the Saudi system continues.

Al-Sharif puts it poignantly when she says, "Driving is not what we are looking for, but being in the driver's seat of our only destiny. That means ending guardianship in Saudi Arabia, which means recognizing women as full citizens."

When the driving ban for women was finally lifted in Saudi Arabia, seven years had passed since Manal al-Sharif uploaded a video of herself driving in Saudi Arabia. Unable to return to her native land, she watched from Australia. She remembered and acknowledged the human rights activists who came before and after her to attempt to lift the driving ban against women. As she had so eloquently written about her experience:

To reach this historic moment, it took nearly three decades from the first attempt to protest the ban: In 1990, 47 women staged a protest drive, after which the religious establishment destroyed their lives and reputations. We all must pay our respects to the women and men who have waged this struggle. Women campaigning to end this ban have lost their freedom, their jobs, have jeopardized their safety, and had their cars confiscated and held. They have been harassed and jailed, and their families have been targeted. They have been called every degrading name and been viciously attacked. They lost their lives as they knew them for daring to drive on the streets of Saudi Arabia.

But no more. Things started to change in 2011, with the start of the #Women2Drive movement. The struggle continued with additional campaigns, including the 2013 campaign led by the Saudi blogger Eman al-Naffan. In 2014, another activist, Loujain al-Hathloul, attempted to cross the Saudi border from the United Arab Emirates by driving

*her car. She was joined by Saudi journalist Maysa al-Amoudi. Both
were arrested and sent to jail for 72 days. Just last month, al-Nafjan
and al-Hathloul were arrested, along with several other women's
rights activists....*

*There can be no modern Saudi kingdom as long as women are still
ruled by men. It may take a long time, but I do believe that kingdom
will come.[44]*

Al-Sharif's acknowledgment of the women who dared to drive in
Saudi Arabia in 1990 highlights two things worthy of note. First, her
actions built upon those of other women before her. At the time, of
course, they had no idea that what they failed to achieve would constitute
the foundation for another woman to begin building upon years later.
Second, what made her campaign successful where previous ones had
failed was the advent of the internet. The internet is also what enabled
Hisham Fageeh's musical satire to be an effective weapon against
inequality. It is the greatest tool mankind has yet developed to spread
"good-idea viruses" and build momentum and support for the concept of
universal human rights.

Capitalizing on Economic Opportunities

Many experts view the lifting of the driving ban as largely an
economic move on Saudi Arabia's part. Since the oil price crisis of 2014,
Saudi Arabia has been working to diversify its economy by attempting
to open itself up to more foreign workers and to tourism. A kingdom
ruled entirely by an authoritarian monarchy has little reason to care about
domestic opinion. But given their depleting oil reserves and the drop
in the price of crude oil, the Saudi monarchy now has a self-interested
reason to care about global opinion and standards.

If private companies can be guilty of "greenwashing" to cover up
corporate misbehavior, then perhaps Saudi Arabia should be called out
for "carwashing"—cynically making a headline-grabbing move that

will allow Saudi women to enter the twentieth century by giving them the right to drive, all the while continuing an otherwise medieval legal system out of the spotlight. Manal al-Sharif is right when she says that "in a society where women aren't free, nobody is free." Among other things, stoning, floggings, amputation of limbs, massive censorship, and public executions for those who seek basic freedom of speech or conscience are still widespread in the kingdom.

At a deeper level, though, the oppressive social and legal systems of Saudi Arabia are reflective of the fact that despite the desire of the kingdom to become a global commerce and tourism destination, it remains one of only a handful of nations in existence in 1948 not to have embraced the Universal Declaration of Human Rights, the most widely accepted and authentically cross-cultural human rights statement that the civilized world has ever produced.

Saudi Arabia's rejection of the UDHR in 1948 was largely due to two of the Declaration's articles: Article 16 and Article 18, which state:

Article 16: (1) Men and women of full age, without any limitation due to race, nationality or religion, have the right to marry and to found a family. They are entitled to equal rights as to marriage, during marriage and at its dissolution.

O

Article 18: Everyone has the right to freedom of thought, conscience and religion; this right includes freedom to change his religion or belief, and freedom, either alone or in community with others and in public or private, to manifest his religion or belief in teaching, practice, worship and observance.

Their rejection of the most fundamental human rights instrument in history makes Saudi Arabia a global outlier. But one could argue that the global community has actually assisted in the maintenance of their oppressive legal system. For example, the profound hypocrisy of electing Saudi Arabia to the UN Women's Rights Commission sends a message that the world approves and sanctions a system where women are clearly second-class citizens.

If Saudi Arabia is acting in its own economic interest at the moment, then this confirms that it will not do any more than is minimally necessary to stave off global opprobrium. So, let's send a clear message that human rights abusers are not welcome in any civilized system that purports to uphold human rights as universal. In short, the global community needs to continue to demand that Saudi Arabia end the deeper theft of legal equality and autonomy for women that is woven into the fabric of Saudi law.

Al-Sharif hopes no one else anywhere in the world will be jailed again and punished simply for driving. The unlikely activist continues to fight to advance women's rights. She is committed to do so until there is full, lasting, and permanent equality for all women in Saudi Arabia.[45]

In response to the lifting of the ban, al-Sharif tweeted, "Saudi Arabia will never be the same again. The rain begins with a single drop." The world must ensure that this first drop starts a deluge in the human rights desert at the heart of the Arab world.

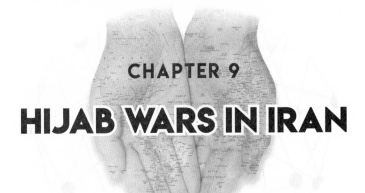

CHAPTER 9

HIJAB WARS IN IRAN

Maedeh Hojabri is an attractive eighteen-year-old gymnast in Iran. Like many girls her age all around the world, she loves to dance. But dancing can be a crime in Iran when you do it on social media.

This past July, Iran's morality police broke into Maedeh's home and arrested her in front of her parents.

Maedeh's crime? She had videotaped herself wearing jeans and a cropped T-shirt, dancing in the privacy of her bedroom. She had then uploaded the videos to Instagram, where her account had three hundred videos and thousands of social media followers.

In Iran there are repressive laws that all their citizens must adhere to concerning both dress and behavior. Under Iran's Islamic Sharia law, dancing is banned. When women are in public they must be dressed modestly and wear a headscarf or a hijab, covering their hair. Beyond this, any display of female beauty is an abomination to the male mullahs, the Shiite clerics who rule the Islamic Republic. If an Iranian citizen crosses their oppressive lines, they can be accused of undermining public decency and arrested. Hojabri's attempt to exercise her fundamental right to freedom of expression drew the ire of the male-dominated Shiite clerical establishment. Although her parents were unaware of her activity on Instagram, her visibility online drew down the full wrath of Iran's mullahs.

Weeks later Hojabri appeared in another video. This time she was not on Instagram. She was on old media: Iranian state TV. And she was wearing the compulsory hijab covering her hair. She publicly confessed that her sexy performances, clothed, but without a hijab, were immoral.

"I had no bad intentions...I did not want to encourage others to do the same," she cried.[46]

Scores of people who watched Hojabri's sobbing statement realized that she was forced to make her confession by Iranian authorities. This provoked a backlash on digital media.

Quickly a hashtag #DancingIsNotaCrime started peppering social media's landscape in support of Hojabri.[47]

Brave Iranian women began posting videos of themselves dancing without their hair covered. They did this to defy the Islamic regime, knowing that they were putting themselves at risk of being arrested. While "access to many social media sites, including Facebook, Twitter, YouTube, and the Telegram messaging app are blocked in Iran...many Iranians evade the filtering through the use of VPN software, which provides encrypted links directly to private networks abroad, and can allow a computer to behave as if it is based in another country."[48]

Next, people from all around the world in places including Finland, Japan, Germany, United States, Canada, and South America joined the Iranian dissidents in solidarity on social media. Globally, men and women were uploading videos of themselves dancing with the hashtag #DancingIsNotaCrime, too. Others mocked Iran's regime by posting favorite music videos from movies like *Footloose* and *Flashdance* at #DancingIsNotaCrime.

But dancing in public is still a crime in today's Iran.

Iran seems to be a perpetual case of the good, the bad, and the ugly. Ugly is the regime, an extremist sectarian system that has caused untold misery to its own people and others by denying basic human rights. Bad is the challenge of dealing with a potential Iranian nuclear weapon.

But there is good, too. The Iranian people increasingly are standing up to their oppressors. Social media has helped to put pressure on the regime to change their laws and allow women in Iran the freedom of expression, the freedom to dance, the freedom to wear a headscarf or the freedom to walk freely with uncovered hair.

That doesn't mean that an Iranian Spring is imminent. However, as resistance to extremist rule grows, so does the possibility of internal regime change, the only kind likely to be permanent.

Four decades after the establishment of Iran's Islamic Republic, more and more Iranian women have seized the power of digital media to demand restoration of the human rights their grandmothers enjoyed before fundamentalist Shiite clerics took power.

Under the pro-American Pahlavi dynasty, which ended with the overthrow of the last shah in 1979, the public wearing of hijabs to cover women's hair had been banned under a 1936 law known as "the unveiling." The elder shah, whose abdication put his son on the throne, was determined to westernize Iran and reform its ancient culture.

Wearing the hijab became optional, as the ban was unenforced by the last shah. His regime also offered women political rights, greater recognition in family law and broader rights to divorce.

Not that there weren't any significant human rights concerns in Iran in those days, but whatever rights Iranian women enjoyed were quashed when, on November 4, 1979, Ayatollah Ruhollah Khomeini and his followers seized power and imposed medieval Islamic law on what had been a fast-developing nation. All of a sudden, the punishment for not wearing a hijab included fines, jail, and lashings. Opponents of the new Ayatollah Khomeini regime were rounded up. Many were beaten, tortured, and publicly executed.

My Stealthy Freedom on Facebook

Before there was Maedeh Hojabri, who wanted to express herself freely in Iran, there was Iranian journalist and human rights activist Masih Alinejad. She was born in 1976, a couple of years before the revolution.

In the pre-digital era women in Iran used whatever limited media that they could to challenge the Islamic regime and advance human rights and women's rights.

Masih Alinejad was one them. In the mid-1990s, when she was eighteen, Masih and a small group of friends painted graffiti on public buildings and produced pamphlets demanding free speech and freedom for political prisoners in Iran.

They were all arrested and spent weeks held incommunicado. Held in filthy jail cells where they were interrogated and forced to betray each other. Some of them were beaten. The students were forced to make videotaped confessions, and the eldest member of the group was hanged.

Alinejad's involvement in the student activist group, leading to their prosecution and sentencing for political subversion, brought an abrupt end to her formal education.

Months later, when Alinejad was released from prison, she got married and then she and her then-husband moved to Tehran. Bored with domestic chores, she sold some of their wedding presents to buy a camera. That camera, over time, would lead to her first media job as a door-to-door market researcher, conducting surveys for the state television station.

Despite Alinejad's lack of formal education, she landed a job as an intern at one of Tehran's reformist newspapers, where her enthusiasm in the pursuit of corruption quickly became apparent.

On her own initiative, she researched and wrote what became a front-page story on a dispute between Iran's president and the Majlis, or parliament. In a matter of months, she was promoted to become the Majlis correspondent for her newspaper and correspondent for a national news agency.

Alinejad had good sources among lawmakers seeking to expose corruption. Her journalistic profile rose. One day, she was talking with two lawmakers in a hallway when a cleric stormed toward her demanding that she cover her hair or he would punch her. Alarmed, she checked her head covering and found that two strands of her hair were exposed.

Alinejad rebuked him for making such an issue of it, but that only enraged him further. Finally, other reporters had to restrain the violent cleric until he could be led away.

In Tehran's political circles, Alinejad remained a gadfly and an annoyance to those in power. After exposing secret payments to members of the Majlis, Alinejad was stripped of her press credentials. Her newspaper and others published front-page stories about the "expelled journalist." Her work for Iran's Fourth Estate continued until her daring reporting during Iran's Green Movement in 2011 led to her having to flee the country. Today she is living in exile in the United States.

A turning point in Alinejad's activism came in 2014 when she posted a picture of herself on Facebook. In the picture, she is outside running down a street lined with pink blossom trees with the brightest smile of happiness. Her long, wavy brown hair, is naturally blowing freely in the wind. While it might not seem significant to those living in the West, for the women in Iran this was both daring and inspiring, considering women are not allowed to go outside without wearing the compulsory hijab.

Alinejad captioned the picture she posted on Facebook and wrote, "Whenever I'm running free and my hair is dancing in the wind, I remember that I am from a country where, for thirty-odd years, my hair has been taken hostage by those in power in the Islamic Republic."

Like all Iranian girls, at the age of seven, Alinejad was forced to cover her hair with a hijab. She, her mother, and her sisters wore head coverings all the time, in the small village where they lived across the towering Alborz Mountains from Tehran—even while they slept.

In Iran, Alinejad's posting prompted an outpouring of approval. Women across the country envied her freedom. They wanted it for themselves. Suddenly she was inspiring thousands of women, so she posted more pictures. She was sure they all had similar pictures of themselves without the hijab, to display what Alinejad called their "stealthy freedom."[49]

She was right. Women in Iran bombarded her Facebook page with pictures and videos of themselves with their hair uncovered. By taking off their hijabs, the brave women risked seventy-four lashes or imprisonment, but a movement was born.

It was a movement Alinejad had not planned, but the response was so massive among her 200,000 Facebook fans, she needed to create a separate page. She called it "My Stealthy Freedom."

"A year after it was created, the Facebook page has more than 760,000 followers and still receives photos from Iran," the UK's *Guardian* reported. "One young woman sent a picture of herself unveiled with a message reading: 'We have never asked to go to heaven by force. Do not turn our lives in this world to hell for the sake of that heaven. We would like to taste the real freedom, not the stealthy one.'"[50,51]

As an exiled journalist, Alinejad keeps shining a light on Iran's compulsory hijab law. In her autobiography, she writes that it was "about much more than hair and dressing modestly, just as Rosa Parks refusing to give her seat to a white man on a bus in Montgomery, Alabama, in 1955 was about more than an unjust seating policy. It's about fighting for what is right."

Every day in Iran is a dangerous day for women, even when they are not showing civil disobedience. In the summer, the morality police arrest or send to court more women for not wearing the hijab than they do in the winter because it is not as easy for the women to stay covered in the intense heat. The Iranian regime actually boasts how they have arrested or sent to court millions of women because of their oppressive hijab laws.

On her two Facebook pages, Alinejad continues to call for the ultimate repeal of Iran's compulsory hijab law as a human rights issue. She writes, "Deciding what you can wear is a form of freedom of speech, and that is a luxury not available in Iran. Compulsory hijab is one of the cornerstones of the Islamic Republic."

She insists that she's not opposed to the hijab itself, but only wants women to be able to choose whether to wear it or not.

Since 2014, "My Stealthy Freedom" has launched several new initiatives, including "White Wednesdays," in which Iranian women are urged to go out in public every Wednesday without hijabs or wearing a white scarf or shawl. She calls white "our color of resistance." Another initiative prompted men to post their own pictures showing support for women's freedom of choice.

She has been condemned by the Iranian regime, but Alinejad is unfazed, humorously calling herself "Iran's master criminal" because of her Facebook page. She told an interviewer, "The Iranian government thinks I have too much hair, too much voice, and I am too much of a woman."

Accepting the 2015 Women's Rights Award at the Summit for Human Rights and Democracy in Geneva, Switzerland, Alinejad lifted a head scarf over her head, calling it "an instrument of oppression against women." She said, "This piece of cloth, in the hands of politicians who do not believe in freedom, is a chain around the necks of Iranian women and over the past thirty-five years has choked their vitality and energy."[52]

The Quietest Protest Sometimes Speaks the Loudest on Social Media

The hijab demonstrations and rebellions on social media also highlight how a particular injustice—in this case the compulsory hijab—can become a lightning rod for opposition to a larger regime of oppression.

In Iran, laws making the hijab mandatory are part of a larger system of legal inequality for women and girls. As the *Washington Post* noted, "Iranian women, for instance, are banned from singing in public, cannot attend public sports events and need a husband's approval to get a passport or travel outside the country."[53] But in 2017, when the Iranian people once again took over Iran's streets to criticize poor living conditions and political oppression, a movement of women who became known as the "Girls of Revolution Street" began to make the compulsory hijab a symbol of their struggle.

Mahatma Gandhi once famously said, "In a gentle way, you can shake the world." Many courageous women in Iran have begun to do precisely that.

Recently, the hijab protests in Iran reached a new level as thirty-one-year-old Vida Movahed, a mother of a toddler, climbed atop a utility box in downtown Tehran. She removed her head scarf and silently waved it on a stick—a peaceful symbol of dissent, dubbed "the quietest protest Iran has ever witnessed" by the *New Yorker*—on Revolution Street.[54] Several people recorded Movahed's protest and sent the video to Alinejad in the United States, who posted it on social media, where it quickly spread.

Movahed was arrested. She was released after an international outcry from individuals and groups, including Amnesty International.

Her daring act prompted other Iranian women to stage similar public protests. At least twenty-nine more women were arrested for their peaceful act of defiance.

Alinejad salutes their bravery, knowing first-hand what Iranian women risk every time they fight for their human rights. As she wrote in her autobiography, "Women in Iran are breaking the law every day just to be themselves."[55]

Incredibly, in 2016 "Iran allocated $1.7 billion for the protection of hijab," while opponents of the law have only their computers, mobile phones, and social media.[56]

Alinejad knows the repeal of Iran's compulsory hijab law may not come quickly, but she is proud that through social media she is putting pressure on the regime, giving Iranian women a voice and, perhaps someday, a choice.

Iranian officials continue to arrest and imprison peaceful protestors, even as these women continue to demonstrate. One compelling image captures a religious woman, wearing a full traditional Iranian chador, mimicking the Girl of Revolution Street's initial protest by waving a headscarf on a stick.[57] This is an incredibly meaningful statement—one that sardonically challenges the regime to answer whether the supposed threat comes from the protests themselves or the garb women are wearing at the time.

These peaceful protests, spread through social media, have raised the profiles of freedom of expression, freedom of conscience, and women's rights around the globe. The Girls of Revolution Street are effectively insisting that the hijab prove its worth. If an item of clothing—or other cultural behavior, for that matter—truly serves a valuable purpose, then let that purpose speak for itself rather than have such attire imposed by panels of male apparel-censors.

Iran's path to better governance remains complicated, the fight will be long, and results remain uncertain. However, the hijab protests are simple yet profound acts that confront the regime in Tehran with the bare truth that as long as Iranian women are forced to wear headscarves, the regime is noticeably wearing nothing at all.

CHAPTER 10

BLOOD DONATION AS A SOCIAL ACTIVITY

It started in 2011, when Karthik Naralasetty, a gifted entrepreneur from Bangalore, India, was reading a news article in an Indian newspaper. It was accompanied by a photograph of a sweet four-year-old girl with big brown eyes and a button nose in a hospital room in rural Karnataka, India. She was receiving a blood transfusion.

The little girl suffered from a chronic blood disease called thalassemia. To stay alive, the little girl's regular treatment required thirty units of blood every month. As Naralasetty would later observe, "That's four gallons of blood every month."

The little girl's family and her doctors constantly have difficulty finding regular blood donors for her life-saving monthly blood transfusions.

Although Naralasetty had not previously heard of thalassemia (a life-threatening hereditary blood disorder) the twenty-two-year-old former student, who had dropped out of Rutgers University in the United States to start his own tech company in India, knew he had to do something to help.

He couldn't understand why in India, with a population of over 1.2 billion people, it was not possible to find regular blood donors for this little girl. So, the entrepreneur started researching the various ways a person could receive blood donations. He discovered that blood donation was a field that needed a digital solution.

According to the World Health Organization, if 1–3 percent of the population in each country donated blood, it would be "enough for the country's need," and there would no longer be blood shortages.[58] Unfortunately, in most countries less than 1 percent of the population takes the time to regularly donate blood.

Part of the problem in some places is a negative stigma attached to donating blood. Some people are too scared of needles to be able to donate. Then there are people who would like to donate, but do not know how to go about it. Sometimes blood may be wasted if it is not managed properly, leading to shortages.

Most people rarely think about donating blood as they go about their daily lives. It is not a burning issue in the headlines demanding immediate attention—until you or one of your loved ones needs a blood transfusion.

Moreover, as Naralasetty soon saw, there is a flawed perception that blood shortages are an issue in underdeveloped nations and not in developed nations, including the United States. The truth is blood shortages remain an issue in both the underdeveloped and developed world.

According to the Red Cross, one blood donation can potentially save up to three lives. Typically, in one session, a donor donates approximately three pints of blood.[59] A person injured in a car accident may need one hundred pints of blood. "Every two seconds someone in the US needs blood."[60]

The dynamics of blood donation also ensure a constant need to renew the existing blood supply. Donated blood must be kept refrigerated and must be used within forty-two days or less. So, even if it's not used, it still must be replaced periodically.

Thus, Naralasetty saw an opportunity to connect people in need with trusted compatible blood donors. As a self-described Facebook addict, who easily jokes about how he logged onto Facebook in 2007 and never logged off, Naralasetty turned to Facebook to develop a network of voluntary blood donors.

In an interview with *The Economist,* Naralasetty said, "If my social networking site can notify me about my friend Raj's birthday why can't it tell me that my friend Raj had an accident and needs three units of blood? I am a heavy Facebook user and it made perfect sense for me to use my network of friends to solve this problem."[61]

His goal was ambitious: "To connect the entire population of Facebook of over a billion people to their blood types and make Facebook the world's largest blood bank."[62] First, he created a group on Facebook for all eight blood types—A+, B+, AB+, O+, A-, B-, AB-, and O-. He linked them together on one website and called it Socialblood. Next, he invited his 1,900 Facebook "friends" to join his Socialblood network.

Incredibly, rapidly, people not only joined, but started sharing requests for blood themselves. Quickly blood donors were being linked up with compatible recipients in their areas. Next, Naralasetty expanded his Socialblood network to include local hospitals and blood banks—first in India, and then around the world.

In one example, a father in India posted a picture of himself with his smiling daughter who had a heart problem and was in urgent need of a blood transfusion. Unfortunately, the hospital could not find any donors for her. "Within twenty-four hours," seventy people, all strangers who lived nearby, reached out to this man and offered to help.

As Naralasetty recounted, "That's the power of Facebook and human connection."

As more and more local and international media outlets reported on Socialblood, his network grew ever wider.[63] Over time, despite some setbacks and challenges, Socialblood expanded from Bangalore, India, to Italy, Australia, Austria, Bangladesh, Brazil, France, Germany, Netherlands, Nigeria, Pakistan, Japan, Spain, Sri Lanka, Sweden, the United Kingdom, and the United States.

By leveraging the power of social media and Facebook's over one billion users, Naralasetty's Socialblood was becoming a platform to crowd-source healthcare.

Inspired by Mahatma Gandhi, who once famously said, "The world has enough for everyone's need, but not enough for everyone's greed," Naralasetty created Socialblood, not to make money, but out of compassion. "Imagine a world where we are connected by blood. All of humanity, mapped to their blood types."[64] His goal is now to build "a movement where we plan to unite a billion people to solve the blood crisis."[65]

#BleedHope

Among Socialblood's crowd-sourcing social media campaigns to encourage people to donate to save the life of another person, is Socialblood's #BleedHope campaign.

By leveraging the power and reach of social media, Socialblood produced a series of powerful short videos of real stories of people who needed blood, could not get it in time, and died.

People like Raheel, a student in his mid-twenties, whose age and good health made him feel invincible—like many people his age. Raheel did not know he had heart disease until he had a heart attack while on a train and needed lifesaving surgery. Raheel did not survive because the local hospital was short of blood.

"Every two seconds somebody needs blood."

Meet a young lady who is madly in love and happy—having just gotten engaged. She and her fiancé, Pooja, are planning the next chapter of their life together. Then one day, while riding their bikes home together, Pooja's bike is hit by a truck. Pooja does not survive to see their wedding day because the local hospital does not have the necessary blood supply.

Like most people, as is human nature, we rarely think it could be us, or one of our loved ones, who one day may need a lifesaving blood transfusion—until it is.

Socialblood is determined to end the blood shortage crisis and is not going to wait for governments to fix this problem. Lives depend on it. At Socialblood, they believe "people can do more for each other than the government can do for us," and they are using digital media and apps to achieve their goal of saving lives.

Today, Naralasetty's Socialblood continues to partner with other groups, hospitals, blood banks, and organizations around the world who share in his mission "to unite humanity in a global effort to transform healthcare, starting with blood." By leveraging the power and reach of digital media, Naralasetty's vision to eliminate the blood crisis once and for all is closer to becoming a reality.

CHAPTER 11

A CHILD'S WISH BECOMES AFRICA'S WISHING WELL

It all began with a little girl's beautifully selfless wish.

Rachel Beckwith had always wanted to help others. In fact, the loving child with a smile that sparkled as brightly as her lovely blue eyes had already proven what a giving soul she was. As a kindergartner, when some parents let their little girls' hair grow long, Rachel convinced her parents to let her cut hers off—donating her dark locks to a charity called Locks of Love, which provides wigs for child cancer patients who've lost their hair to chemo. Rachel was in the process of growing her hair out again so she could repeat that selfless act as she approached her ninth birthday.[66]

Still, much to her parents' awe and delight, this little girl wanted to do more. It was in her church where an international cause would capture the attention of her compassionate heart for the first time. While listening to her pastor's sermon one day, Rachel learned that children in Africa and in many other parts of the world lack something that she, like most Americans, had always taken for granted: clean drinking water. She learned that her church, just outside of Seattle, had been actively raising money to bring clean water to those in need through a nonprofit organization called charity: water.[67] So Rachel asked her parents if she could get involved. They went online and investigated together, and before long, Rachel made up her mind. Instead of asking for presents to celebrate her ninth year, she would ask everyone she knew to donate nine dollars to her personal charity: water campaign (charitywater.org/Rachel). The website made it easy.[68] She could promote her personal campaign through her parents' Facebook pages or email and accept payments via credit cards or PayPal. It's a type of fundraising that was unimaginable to anyone in her parents' generation, who had grown up knocking on doors selling Cub Scout Pens or Girl Scout Cookies in nothing wider than a neighborhood's radius. But Rachel was able to get her campaign up and running in a matter of minutes, and she didn't see any reason not to set a lofty goal of $300.

By the time her birthday came around on July 12, 2011, Rachel had only raised $220. So, she was actively thinking of ways she could continue to raise money for the cause when, eight days later, a truck on the highway struck her family's car. In the thirteen-car pileup that resulted, Rachel's mom, dad, and siblings miraculously walked away. Rachel did not. She suffered life-threatening injuries.

Prayers went up. Word spread in the Seattle area of the little girl with the big heart, and in a sign of support for Rachel's recovery, hundreds of local citizens logged on to Rachel's charity: water campaign and made donations. The thought from many in the community was that while they might not be able to do anything to help Rachel directly, the least they could do was to help raise her spirits by fulfilling her selfless wish.

Within a day or two, Rachel surpassed her $300 goal. Money poured in from local residents. And then something bigger happened: Through the power of the World Wide Web, the vast reach of Twitter, the borderless friendships of Facebook, and more, Rachel's story began to spread. Donations poured in from thousands of people, all across the country. Some came in the form of large gifts, but many came in the form of small donations. Other children heard about the story and emptied their piggy banks in Rachel's name. In fact, donations began to pour in from around the world, including some from Africa, where the story of this little American girl who thought enough to do something for the children of their continent began to spread.

In a matter of days, Rachel's family would gather at her bedside and share the news that she had raised more than $47,000 for the cause she cared so much about. Whether or not she heard the news, the family would never know. Rachel didn't make it. There was no chance of her recovery, and her parents made the impossibly difficult choice to remove her from life support.

Even then, Rachel's wish lived on. Through the power of the Web, Rachel raised over $800,000 that summer—and that was before Nicholas Kristof wrote a column about Rachel in *The New York Times*, after which other traditional media outlets began spreading Rachel's story far and wide.[69]

By the end of 2011, Rachel's campaign had raised more than $1.2 million for charity: water—100 percent of which was used to build wells. Rachel's wish led to the installation of fresh-water wells in 143 villages in Ethiopia, providing clean water to more than 37,000 people.

"*Rachel's Gift*, the video that tells Rachel's story, has been watched by more than 600,000 viewers on Vimeo," says Scott Harrison, charity: water's founder. And it's still going strong.

In 2012, Harrison took Rachel's mother to Ethiopia to see first-hand the wells Rachel's campaign built. They documented that trip with a digital video camera, posted it as a follow-up story on the charity: water website, and the story spread even further. Each quarter since, Rachel's mother has started a new fundraising campaign in Rachel's name, and in the third quarter of 2013 alone, Rachel was able to raise an additional $22,363 for the cause—surpassing a lofty $20,000 goal her mother set—primarily through the spread of her story through social media and the instantaneous ability the Web provides for individuals to make donations the moment they're moved to do so.

Rachel's is one of hundreds of stories that have helped turn charity: water into a modern-day beacon of hope, not only for nonprofits looking to spread their messages and raise much needed funds, but for people all over the earth who are desperately in need of help to acquire the necessities of life.

The Universal Declaration of Human Rights does not name "clean water" specifically as a right. Yet the document certainly implies the right to safe drinking water in Article 25:

(1) Everyone has the right to a standard of living adequate for the health and well-being of himself and of his family, including food, clothing, housing and medical care and necessary social services, and the right to security in the event of unemployment, sickness, disability, widowhood, old age or other lack of livelihood in circumstances beyond his control.

(2) Motherhood and childhood are entitled to special care and assistance. All children, whether born in or out of wedlock, shall enjoy the same social protection.

In fact, in February of 2011, the United Nations declared 2013 the "International Year of Water Cooperation."[70] In so doing, part of the organization's campaign "highlights water as being at the core of sustainable development," to include "safe drinking water and sanitation."

Other than the air we breathe, it is difficult to think of anything that is more fundamental to life itself than clean water. Harrison says to that notion: "The fact that 800 million people today don't have access to something most people take for granted is an absolute injustice."

Harrison's organization points out that it is not uncommon for villagers in Africa to have to walk for miles just to get back and forth to any source of water. Even after walking all that way, a mother could wind up waiting in line for eight hours at a well that's serving a large region. "Forty billion hours are wasted in Africa every year fetching water—and these mothers go about getting it, knowing that that water may be tainted and kill their children anyway. It's one of the greatest injustices in the world."

CHAPTER 12

WISHING WELL TAPS A GLOBAL DIGITAL RESERVOIR

S cott Harrison, charity: water's founder, isn't one to be discouraged by obstacles. His organization's goal is overtly and purposefully optimistic: "To bring clean and safe drinking water to every person on the planet." Part of the way in which he's accomplishing that task is by telling powerful, uplifting stories of charity: water's progress and success on the Web.

Harrison knows a thing or two about promotion. He was an extremely successful nightclub and fashion-event promoter in New York City before he decided to leave that notorious world behind and embark on a mission for good. He turned all of his expertise in drawing crowds, media attention, and celebrities together into doing something to provide clean drinking water to the poor of Ethiopia.[71]

When it comes to fundraising from the public, much of that mission has been carried out online, going back to charity: water's very beginnings in 2006. Charity: water was the first nonprofit organization to reach a million followers on Twitter; they were also the first charity to open an Instagram account.

"It's really the content and the story that matters," Harrison says. "Social media is just a tool." The stories that used to be told in brochures and pamphlets and newspaper articles can now be told through digital video and shared instantly with millions. The world of media-delivery has changed in recent years, so Harrison made sure his organization harnessed the full potential of those changes. "And if the world changes again, we'll try to continue to tell stories using whatever tools are available to us."

As fundraisers, Harrison says, "We're visual storytellers. We believe in showing, not telling. That's why Instagram, which wasn't embraced by a lot of other charities early on, has really been our sweet spot. It's a place where we get to communicate the joy of clean water in pictures and communicate the need, as well."

To put it in philosophical terms, Harrison quotes Aristotle: "The soul never thinks without a picture."

By using the charity: water website, Instagram, Twitter, Facebook, and more, Harrison's team have managed to elicit donations—and the engaged awareness those donations imply—from more than 37,000 individual fundraisers, funding more than 9,000 water projects in twenty countries.

"We are all about the picture: This is the picture of the need, this is a picture of the solution, and this is a picture of the hope and joy that comes through helping and serving."

Online, the proverbial picture that is worth a thousand words can be shared many millions of times; and a video can move thousands of people to help fund a solution. Thanks to the rapidly advancing technologies of digital video cameras and editing software, "The cost of making videos has come down dramatically," Harrison notes. What used to involve whole camera and sound crews, and editing suites, and potentially thousands of dollars per minute, can now be done by an individual and a laptop. "We use a camera that only cost a few thousand dollars to make all of our in-house videos—videos that are cinematic in look, and remarkably powerful, given their short length—for a Web-friendly audience."

"It's amazing what we can do with so little resources. The Rachel video, in fact, was shot with that $2,200 camera, edited the following the day, and uploaded. That's it. No one has touched it since. And yet, it's been shared and viewed again and again and again."

The power of emotion, shared through the power of technology, is a combination whose impact should not be underestimated.

And it doesn't stop there. Anyone who donates to charity: water can see where their money goes by clicking on a map of the organization's clean-water projects around the world. A person who donated to Rachel's birthday fundraiser can click on a map of Ethiopia and actually see the exact locations of the wells that were built with those funds. Click again and another video shows Rachel's mother's journey to Ethiopia, where viewers can meet the children who are alive thanks to the access to clean water that her daughter made possible or see Rachel's picture enshrined on the altar of a Catholic church in a country thousands of miles from Rachel's home.

Connecting the public to photos and videos of the charity: water mission in action on their website and via social media is only part of the story when it comes to technology's effects on Harrison's endeavors. In December 2012, charity: water won a $5 million grant from Google's Global Impact Awards to develop low-cost, wireless well-monitoring technologies.

"It's an incredible design challenge," Harrison says. "How do you power, protect, transmit, and measure the flow of water in these wells, and do that for under $200." The task is being accomplished through the cooperation of tech companies in China, Spain, and right here in Silicon Valley. "We're confident that we're going to finally arrive at a solution," he says, which will not only allow charity: water to better monitor and maintain the wells they install, but will provide data the world has never seen before. While there are estimates that 30 to 40 percent of the world's wells aren't functioning properly at any given time, no one has been able to monitor the thousands of wells in remote areas. So no real data exists.

"In the meantime, we've implemented a human system of post-implementation monitoring in Ethiopia, visiting over 2,000 charity: water projects twice a year with trained mechanics. We bought them motorcycles so they can get around easier. So, they'll be covering 100 percent of our work in Ethiopia over the next six months. When that's done, we will have a bigger data set on performances of water projects than has ever existed."

Just imagine what the data set on countless wells, delivered wirelessly, could bring to the world's water supply once the technology is put in place. Charity: water (and other organizations, both governmental and non-governmental) will be able to gather instant feedback, and potentially put a stop to dangerous conditions, should a well malfunction, *before* sickness and deaths occur. Adjustments can be made in manufacturing and supply chains in order to quickly get needed well and pump parts where they're needed most. And as the data and resources are shared, the whole dynamic of distributing water to those who need it could be changed for the better forever.

Success in all areas won't come overnight. But thanks to technology, it appears that it's coming faster than anyone ever could have imagined until the last few years of human history.

"We've got a big problem. Eight hundred million people without clean water," Harrison says. "But," he adds in a voice that is simultaneously humble and confident, and so emblematic of this new era of human freedom, "We're working on it."

CHAPTER 13

FREEING MINDS ONE NOSE DRIVE AT A TIME

When Kim Jong-un's dictatorship in *Pyongyang* summoned Thae Yong-ho back to North Korea after being stationed in London for three years, he knew he could not return.

Instead, the deputy ambassador to the United Kingdom from North Korea made the dangerous decision to defect to South Korea with his wife and children.

Thae had studied international politics in Pyongyang and Beijing universities. Prior to serving in London, he had been posted in Demark, where one of his sons was born, and then stationed in Sweden. While spending almost half his life outside of North Korea, every day had been like living a double life in a precarious balancing act. On one hand, Thae had to serve North Korea's tyrannical communist regime with his daily reports to Pyongyang. On the other hand, Thae was enjoying the freedoms and human rights in the countries where he was posted—while knowing his countrymen were being oppressed back home.

As the former high-ranking North Korean diplomat explained during an interview in 2017 with CNN's Christiane Amanpour, Thae said, "Mainly, I did not want to let my sons lead a life like me, which is nothing but a modern slave."[72]

North Korea, officially known as the Democratic People's Republic of Korea (DPRK), has been ruled by a seventy-year-old totalitarian regime. Supreme leader Kim Jong-un is the latest dictator in the Kim "Great Successor" family line of North Korea, where unquestioned loyalty is demanded and systematic human rights violations occur daily.

Totalitarianism is a form of government that denies all fundamental human rights by totally subordinating people to the state. Italian dictator Benito Mussolini coined the term *totalitario* in the early 1920s to characterize the new fascist state of Italy, which he further described as "all within the state, none outside the state, none against the state." By the beginning of World War II, "totalitarian" had become synonymous with absolute and oppressive single-party government.

The Korean War (1950–1953) began on June 25, 1950, when soldiers and tanks of the North Korean Army poured across the 38th parallel in a surprise invasion of South Korea. At the end of the Second World War, the Korean peninsula had been divided approximately in half along the 38th parallel. This became the de facto border between communist North Korea, backed by the Soviets and Chinese, and South Korea, supported by the United States and other western allied powers. United Nations forces from over a dozen allied countries entered the war on South Korea's behalf that July in an effort to repel the invading force from the north.

When the war ended, approximately five million soldiers and civilians had lost their lives. Today, the Korean peninsula remains divided in a long-standing ceasefire where the threat of a catastrophic war breaking out looms like a dark cloud.[73] Indeed, the Kim regime has masterfully played on that threat for decades in an effort to extort financial and other assistance from both South Korea and other nations of the world.

In the closed and tightly-controlled society of North Korea, sometimes it seems as if time has stood still. Most people do not have cars. The roads are peppered with checkpoints—mostly used by bicycles. Most North Koreans cannot simply go to a grocery store that is stocked with the food readily available in most countries. In fact, starvation is an omnipresent problem in a nation that suffers from famine and lives under heavy economic sanctions. For years, different countries have sanctioned North Korea in an attempt to deter North Korea's rogue regime from pouring whatever resources they have into building ballistic and nuclear weapons, while threatening different regions in the world.

Political freedom and freedom of speech are nonexistent in North Korea. The only news media the North Koreans have access to is state-controlled. Moreover, North Korea does not have the internet. As a result, the population of North Korea lives inside one of the most isolated and backward nations on Earth.

Malnutrition is so rampant in North Korea that the mental and physical growth of many North Korean children is stunted. Moreover, periodic episodes of famine have resulted in outbreaks of mass starvation. Few outsiders have seen the horrific effects of these tragic realities, but those who have report seeing many people—including children—dying in public with others reduced to eating grass and tree bark in an effort to survive.

Although it shocks the mind of most outsiders, such malnutrition and mass starvation are not the result of natural disaster but rather a deliberate policy by the North Korean regime to minimize the possibility of popular resistance while channeling food reserves to the military and political elite.

North Korea has a state-imposed cult of veneration for the Kim family where citizens are required to honor the Kims in many of the ways normally associated with religious worship. The simple act of criticizing the Kim regime can lead to arrest and harsh sentences in a vast system of prison labor camps modeled on the infamous Gulag system of Stalinist Russia. Although the full extent of the North Korea prison camp system remains hidden from the outside world, the small number of survivors who have escaped tell of systematic slavery, rape, starvation, torture, medical experimentation, and mass murder as brutal as the concentration camps of Nazi Germany.

North Korea has used prisoners to test the lethality of the chemical, biological, and nuclear weapons that they employ to threaten the rest of the world. Moreover, North Korea practices a uniquely evil and depraved system of multigenerational punishment. Children are incarcerated with their parents—leading to multiple generations of prisoners who have never known life outside of the camps. Entire families are also tortured and executed together as punishment in the camps.

Outside of this vast prison camp system, the government actively encourages citizens to report neighbors who are not patriotic and loyal to the Kim dynasty. Arbitrary detentions, public executions, and forced labor infuse submission and conformity among the populace. These dehumanizing tactics systematically employed by the Kim regime maintain a cruel and brutal climate of total state control over the North Koreans.

By closing the door to the rest of the world, and by keeping the entire population of North Korea malnourished and uninformed as to life outside of their borders, the Kim regime keeps the citizens loyal and dependent.

Since defecting, Thae wants to help free North Koreans from such oppression. But how does one go about undermining a tyrannical regime that has been in power for over six decades in a notoriously isolated nation?

By smuggling in and disseminating "outside information" inside North Korea. Such information can help to free the minds of North Korean citizens by discrediting the propaganda of the regime and introducing concepts that are nonexistent in North Korean society. For example, North Korean defectors have said that films about love between men and women—common in the free world—can be highly subversive in a society where most citizens are taught to only express love for the "supreme leader." Most North Koreans have been taught that theirs is a prosperous society—with citizens of other countries such as South Korea living in relative poverty. So television programs and films that show the level of material prosperity of citizens in Seoul—only a few miles away—can profoundly undermine the legitimacy of the North Korean regime. Indeed, even the basic notion of freedom itself can be highly subversive in a society where human lives are only valued based on their usefulness to the regime.

Enter the data-smuggling potential of digital media in the form of USB drives and SD cards.

During a panel discussion at the Center for Strategic & International Studies, Thae emphasized how critical it is to engage with North Korea's population of about twenty-four million people by using the "soft power" of information. By using a soft power approach via digital media—specifically USB and SD cards, which are called "nose cards" in North Korea—outside information can be smuggled into North Korea.

As Thae explains, "If somebody wants to search your body whether you have any USBs or whatever, the boys instantly take it out and they put it in their nose…In Korean terms, we call it 'ko kadeu' card, that is nose card."

With the technological advances in the past five years, these nose cards may hold hours of television, music, movies, news, and education programming from the outside world. They can be played on phones, computers, and other devices in North Korea even without access to the internet.

The key, Thae emphasizes, to breaking through the rogue regime's hold on the minds of the people is the type of content that is smuggled in through digital media. It must be tailored-made to cause North Koreans to question their regime when they are able to see the world outside of their borders.

For instance, Thae points out that in North Korea there is no concept or sense of payment for their labor. North Koreans need to be educated that they should be paid for the work that they do. This is the beginning of breaking the psychology that has allowed so many generations of North Koreans to accept a status of slavery to the state.

"We should start from these basic concepts," Thae says. "Not 'Oh, Kim Jong-un is a dictator,' or 'North Korea is communist society,' or whatever. We should start from basic concepts of human rights and freedom."[74]

To further demonstrate his point, Thae shared a story illustrating acceptable norms in North Korea regarding women's rights.

In North Korea, if a girl is physically beautiful, then naturally when you reach at the age of 14, you are registered by the Party and People's Committee of that region. And if that girl's physical beauty continues to the age of 16 or 17, then the girl would be sent by the authority to Pyongyang to either work in a special guesthouse or in special hospitals for senior leaders. That kind of thing was common in Lee Dynasty. But what is the general concept of normal people? For instance, in the countryside village, if the girl was sent by the authority to the capital for that kind of purpose, then North Korean—the normal North Korean population accept it as a kind of honor. They do not think that this is a human rights violation or the sexual abuse or sexual exploitation. No, they accept it as a kind of honor of the family to be sent from countryside to the capital.

Thae believes that only when North Koreans understand that they have a right to be treated as more than objects by those in power will they begin to resist such exploitation—and every other form of state abuse forced upon citizens by the North Korean regime.

Thae also believes the North Koreans are increasingly growing dissatisfied with their leadership. Year after year they watch Supreme Leader Kim Jung-un continue to spend state funds on nuclear and military arsenal while many North Koreans either starve or live in a state of near starvation. It is reported that in North Korea, approximately 40 percent of the population live below the poverty line.

Now, more than ever, it is possible to bring the liberating ideas of freedom, human dignity, and basic rights to even the darkest and most oppressive societies on the earth.

CHAPTER 14

CYBER-ACTIVISM IN A LAND WITHOUT INTERNET

A t Dalhousie University, in Halifax, Nova Scotia, in Canada, there are some very strange donation boxes on campus. These boxes do not ask for typical donations of books or clothing. Instead, plastered on the boxes is a poster of North Korea's Supreme Leader Kim Jong-Un's face. His mouth has been symbolically cut out into a USB port, a slot that is large enough to slip in flash drives, USB drives, and thumb drives into the donation boxes.

In part, the poster simply states:

Want to help educate the people of North Korea about life outside the regime?

Donate your new or used (4GB) USBs to No Chain for North Korea.

All USBs will be erased and downloaded with South Korean media and either dropped into North Korea via drones, balloons or bottles.

As Canada's CBC News's *The National* reported at the time,

A small army of activists in Halifax is infiltrating North Korea one USB drive at a time. It's all about getting tiny pieces of information into a country that tries to shelter its population from the outside world. Students at Dalhousie University are making videos of life in Halifax and putting them on the USB drives. They are then sent to South Korea where they are put in bottles of rice and dropped in the ocean—set adrift to North Korea where they are sold on the black market, intended for the population there to see something that is otherwise forbidden: images of what freedom looks like.[75]

The Flash Drives for Freedom project at Dalhousie is a collaboration between the Human Rights Foundation, Forum 280, USB Memory Direct, and their partners.

Flash Drives for Freedom's mission is to "significantly increase the capacities of North Korean defector groups." As their mission statement explains: "Believe it or not, USBs are a significant form of sharing information in North Korea. Many citizens have devices with USB ports. So for many years, North Korean defectors have organized efforts to smuggle outside info into North Korea on USB drives to counter Kim Jong-un's constant propaganda."[76]

One of the defector groups is called "No Chain for North Korea." On January 31, 2018, Jung Gwang-Il, a North Korean defector, and the founder of "No Chain for North Korea," went to Dalhousie University in Canada with his "plea to help his home country." He took his campaign of using digital media to help free the citizens of North Korea to the students with the assistance of Dalhousie's associate professor of International Development Studies, Robert Huish, an expert on North Korea.[77]

According to Jung, "No Chain for North Korea" is a play on words. He views "DPRK as a giant prison camp that binds its people in chains."[78] Jung would know. As reported by the *Mic Network's* Kelly Kasulis in "I spent a day with North Korean defectors, who lived through hell and want a revolution":

In North Korea, Jung lived as a trader who was occasionally allowed to visit China—there, he watched South Korean dramas for the first time. During North Korea's "arduous march" famine, in the 1990s, Jung said he regularly saw officers stacking bodies of starved children on his morning walk to work. Both circumstances fueled his skepticism of the Kim regime's propaganda, but a wrongful prison sentence was what pushed him to defect.

In 1999, a co-worker accused him of espionage. He was innocent, but that didn't matter: In the middle of the night, officers showed up at Jung's house to beat and arrest him without explanation. After ten months of torment in a prison—his arms tied behind his back in a crouching "pigeon torture" position—he finally confessed to a crime he never committed. During those ten months, he says he dropped from 165 pounds to roughly 79 or 80. "I was not able to hold myself up on my own," he recounted at the 2016 Oslo Freedom Forum.[79]

Jung then spent more than two years at Yodok—one of North Korea's many known prison camps, which are often compared to Hitler's concentration camps or Lenin's gulags. He worked sixteen hours a day for more than two years. In the winters, dead bodies of other prisoners would freeze into a "big, jellied block of flesh," and he'd have to break them apart using a shovel before burying them.

He was released in April 2003, when authorities determined the charges against him were false. But Jung couldn't take it anymore. Twelve days later, he risked his life to swim across the Tumen River into China—an escape plan that's getting even harder to pull off these days. He crossed into Vietnam, then Cambodia, then Thailand and eventually settled in South Korea.[80]

Among Jung's hopes for North Koreans is the goal of seeing the nation's infamous system of prison camps destroyed in his lifetime.

Cyber-Activism

In North Korea, cyber-activism is described as activism carried out through digitally distributed information. Jung is convinced that when the citizens of North Korea, through these digital media campaigns, see how good and how free life is in other countries, they will want the same freedoms.

There are other groups who do this, too, but what is unique about Jung's effort is his specific approach. He had seen a story about Amazon. com that inspired him to try using drones. At the time, Amazon was testing drones to use them as a means of delivery for their goods. If Amazon could use drones for this, Jung thought, why couldn't he use them to bring in digital media with downloaded information that could help free the minds of North Koreans?[81]

Previously, despite it being illegal to listen to foreign radio stations in North Korea, defectors used radio and short wave broadcasts to attempt to increase the information flow to North Koreans from the outside world. Unfortunately, radio transmissions can be jammed. BBC News recently encountered this barrier when Kim Jong-Un's regime quickly and "aggressively" jammed a new BBC radio service directed into the Korean peninsula.[82]

For many years, activists sought to smuggle information into North Korea by using balloons with leaflets inside. While gauging weather and wind patterns, the activists would release the balloons from South Korea's border, with the hope that the balloons would float across the border into North Korea. But now, the advancements of digital media and drone technology has opened up many new possibilities for disseminating information from the outside world into North Korea.

Back in Canada, the students of Dalhousie University have made videos to download onto USB (flash or thumb) drives. They want to show North Koreans what an average student in Halifax would do in their everyday life. The next step in this "soft power" information warfare campaign against the Kim Jong-un totalitarian regime is for students to edit the videos into small files and download them onto the donated digital media.

The downloaded drives are sent to South Korea, where Jung and his network of other defectors and activists put them into empty water bottles. The human rights activists often add a few US dollars for good measure. Then they wait at the border of South Korea until the tide is just right. They then throw the bottles into the water to be carried toward fisherman in North Korea.

These bottles of hope also contain rice as a testament to the humanitarian motives of the senders. This is important given that food in North Korea is so scarce. Additionally, the fisherman who find the bottles can also sell the drives on the black market and thereby earn enough money to feed their families for months.

These bottles may not appear to be a menacing threat to the Kim regime, as they bob up and down, pushed along by the tide. But as Jung says, "Outside information is the greatest fear among dictators." No wonder oppressive regimes such a North Korea devote so much effort to keeping their citizens in a state of ignorance. Totalitarian regimes know better than most the truth of the adage that "knowledge is power." And the Digital Age is giving us an expanding array of ways to press the knowledge of freedom and universal rights into the most hellish places on Earth. If the chains of mental bondage can be broken in the Hermit Kingdom, then they can be broken anywhere on Earth.

CHAPTER 15

FIGHTING TERRORISTS WITH FACEBOOK

It was February 2002, and Facebook had not been invented yet when the French-Colombian politician, Ingrid Betancourt, was campaigning for president of Colombia.

The author of the best-selling autobiography in France, *La Rage Au Coeur—Rage in the Heart*, chronicling her fight against corruption as a Colombian senator—was in a region in Southern Colombia that was controlled by Marxists guerrillas. It was not safe.

In fact, it was downright dangerous. Three years of intense negotiations and peace talks between the Colombian government and the FARC had recently collapsed.

FARC is the Spanish abbreviation for the "*Fuerzas Armadas Revolucionarias de Colombia*," which translates to the "Revolutionary Armed Forces of Colombia." Connected to Soviet-influenced communist movements, the Marxist rebel group was initially formed by communist farmers in central Colombia.

FARC grew out of the decade-long civil war in Colombia known as *La Violencia*: The Violence. Much of FARC had originated from La Violencia's "resistance committees."[83]

FARC opposed any outside influence from multinational companies and foreign governments in Colombia's affairs. Their mission was to redistribute the wealth from the wealthy to the poor in a country historically plagued by high levels of inequality. It soon turned violent.

"FARC has carried out bombings, assassinations, hijackings, and other armed attacks against various political and economic targets in the country; it has also kidnapped foreigners for ransom, executing many of its captives. The FARC's links to drug trafficking have brought hundreds of millions of dollars annually into the organization from taxes it imposes."[84]

As Betancourt was heading for the town of San Vicente del Caguán with her campaign manager, Clara Rojos, armed FARC guerrillas surrounded them. The women were snatched from their car and kidnapped.

The presidential hopeful and her campaign manager were forcibly taken deep into Colombia's rainforest jungle, thick with brush, trees, and vegetation that is so dense one cannot see the ground by aircraft flying overhead and little to no sunlight can pass through it.

For over five years, FARC held the hostages captive in unimaginable conditions and denied their prisoners any human rights. To punish, control, and subdue a hostage, FARC would chain captives to a tree or to each other. Privacy was nonexistent, communication forbidden. Rarely was clean water available to the captives, who barely survived on beans and rice. To fend off possible rescue missions, and to avoid army patrols, FARC would move hostages by forcing them to march chained together in sweltering heat from one guerilla camp to another.

Since FARC'S inception, it had kidnapped over 700 hostages, some of whom they held captive for over ten years. Not surprisingly, thirty-one countries had designated the group as a terrorist organization.

When Facebook was founded in 2004 in the United States, Ingrid Betancourt, Clara Rojos, and other hostages were already being held by FARC deep in Colombia's dense rainforest jungle. And as Facebook was growing by leaps and bounds, connecting people all over the world, including in Colombia, FARC continued to hold its hostages captive and to terrorize the country.

Meet Oscar Morales

There was not a time in Oscar Morales's life when FARC had not been waging what became the longest-running armed insurgency in the Americas. Morales, a Colombian native who graduated college when he was twenty-one years old, became a civil engineer. He had taken an early interest in the internet's nascent days in the mid-1990s when he became a self-described "computer geek."

While he loathed the chaos and terrifying disruptions caused by FARC in his homeland, he did not know of a way he could do anything about it. That quickly changed when a shocking news story broke about one of FARC's hostages—Clara Rojos, Ingrid Betancourt's campaign manager; she had given birth to a boy named Emmanuel while in captivity, and FARC guerillas had separated mother from child.

As *The New York Times*'s Simon Romero reported:

> *Emmanuel's existence was first reported to an unsettled public last year. But revelations in recent weeks, including his name, obtained from an emaciated police officer who spent 17 days in the wilderness after escaping from a guerrilla encampment in southern Colombia, have shaken a country hardened by a seemingly interminable war in which kidnapping has been polished into an effective weapon.*

The policeman, John Frank Pinchao, who had been able to flee from FARC, described how horribly Clara had suffered in captivity. He could hear Clara asking to be able to see her son, whom the guerrillas had now been raising for some time.[85]

For a nation already suffering trauma from years of kidnappings, bombings, and assassinations, it was too much to fathom. The conflict had degraded into such a gut-wrenching, stomach-turning form, it could not be tolerated in a civil society. What kind of a country permits a child born in captivity to be separated from his mother?

"If Emmanuel dies," Héctor Abad Faciolince, one of Colombia's most prominent novelists, wrote in a widely reported essay, the country is in deep trouble. "If Emmanuel doesn't start school and doesn't grow healthy and strong, we will be the most savage country on Earth, the dirtiest, the worst."

Morales, the self-described computer geek, had had it with FARC. He knew he had to do something. That's when he turned to Facebook, then just a relatively new social media company. It was on January 4, 2008, when Morales created a Facebook group called One Million Voices Against FARC, which highlighted the atrocities of the group.

As David D. Burstein in *Fast Company* reported, "The group was dedicated to bringing down FARC and to demanding the release of several hundred hostages. Just hours after the Facebook group launched, Morales watched the membership climb to 1,500 members. The next day there were 4,000. By the end of the first week: 100,000."[86] Within several days, in a purported humanitarian gesture, FARC agreed to release Clara Rojos's son, Emmanuel, who was now three years old, and one other hostage.

As the One Million Voices Against FARC Facebook membership grew, people from around the world began contacting Morales and offering to help. Morales also used his Facebook page to organize mass protests against the terrorist group.

The unassuming geek, who originally thought he was voicing his opposition to FARC online with some friends, had no idea that his actions would have such far-reaching consequences. In this respect, Morales should be an encouragement to us all. He did not know if it could make a difference, but he felt he had to try. Fortunately, thanks to the power of social media, he founded a movement. Morales was able to effect real change on the ground by igniting a peaceful public revolution against FARC.

On February 4, 2008, in twenty-seven cities throughout Colombia and 104 cities around the world, millions of people took to the streets and marched against FARC. "No more kidnappings! No more lies! No more deaths! No more FARC!" shouted some of the protestors. It was the largest protest in Colombia's history.[87]

When social media is used by individuals like Oscar Morales, it has the potential to overcome evil and advance the cause of human rights. Too often, revolution is a strategy employed by the violent few to oppress the many. But Oscar Morales proved to be a revolutionary for good who ignited a firestorm of public outrage against the worst excesses of FARC. By using digital media to effect change, Morales's One Million Voices Against FARC helped inspire a nation to stand up to a terrorist organization in a way that brought out the best in the people of Colombia.

CHAPTER 16

THE PLAGUE OF MODERN-DAY SLAVERY

In its most basic form, slavery occurs when one person is owned and controlled by another person for that other person's personal gain and/or gratification. In violation of their dignity as human beings, men, women, and children who are enslaved are deprived of their freedom and treated as property.

Throughout history, slavery has taken on many evil and reprehensible forms, from forced labor to today's modern-day sex trade and human trafficking.

Abraham Lincoln, the 16th president of the United States, began the process of making slavery illegal in the United States when he signed the Emancipation Proclamation in 1862. Facing public opposition in the North and open hostility in the South, he said, "I never, in my life, felt more certain that I was doing right, than I do in signing this paper."[88]

While the Emancipation Proclamation may have declared Southern slaves to be free, it did not stop slavery from happening in America. To finish the job once the Civil War was over, Lincoln helped to push the 13th Amendment through Congress. This historic amendment to the US Constitution permanently outlawed slavery throughout the country.

Tragically, despite all of these victories, a deeply depraved and exploitative slavery that we now refer to as "human trafficking" continues to victimize the most vulnerable among us—both in the United States and around the world.

It is estimated that there are nearly thirty million slaves in the world today. Men, women, and children, who are forced to work and barely subsist, live in constant fear and are frequently subjected to all kinds of exploitative, horrific sexual abuse.

The freedoms and protections contained in the Bill of Rights, the first ten amendments of the US Constitution, have been germane to many declarations of human rights, including the Universal Declaration of Human Rights. Sometimes called a "Bill of Rights for humanity," the Universal Declaration explicitly condemns the practice of slavery. Article 4 states: "No one shall be held in slavery or servitude; slavery and the slave trade shall be prohibited in all their forms."

Nonetheless, the modern slave trade of human trafficking remains a huge global problem. While not legal in most countries of the world, slavery is still highly prevalent and believed to be one of the world's fastest-growing criminal activities. Sadly, and tragically, it is estimated that there are now more people enslaved through human trafficking worldwide than during the entire era of slavery in America.

In the West, the most popular forms of human trafficking are involuntary domestic servitude and sex trafficking. According to UNICEF—the United Nations International Children's Emergency Fund—as many as two million children have been forced into prostitution. The perpetrators of modern-day slavery use various methods of violence, coercion, drug use and addiction, deception, force, and manipulation to control their victims.

In 2013, the US government estimated that at any given time, approximately twenty-seven million men, women, and children may have been victims of human trafficking. Within that twenty-seven million, 18,000 people from over fifty countries are trafficked into the United States every year and over 300,000 children are trafficked within the United States annually.

Even in Atlanta, a cradle of the civil rights movement, the practice is festering. The FBI has identified Atlanta as having one of the largest sex-trafficking industries in the United States, with nearly half the victims being underage and subjected to sexual exploitation.

Those are cold, hard statistics. They're important to know, but mere numbers cannot convey the horrors and terror that victims of human trafficking are forced to endure, or the pain and suffering they experience.

Many of the victims of human trafficking are young teenage girls. Older men play on their gullibility and desire for romance and adventure. The perpetrator is a predator and may take his time, patiently discussing a young girl's problems and listening to her dreams until she becomes infatuated with him.

She may have stars in her eyes and want to be a pop singer, or a movie star, or meet famous celebrities, or travel overseas to romantic or exotic places. The perpetrator will promise to help her achieve her dreams and may convince her to run away with him so that she can be free of the restrictions her parents and other adults place on her.

Eventually, the young girl's naiveté and vulnerability leads her into the inexorable clutches of a sex-trafficking ring. Within hours of running away with what turns out to be a manipulative and menacing pimp, she may find herself coerced into working as a labor or sex slave in a major city.

Twenty years ago, there were no anti-trafficking laws in place. In one case, a pimp who raped and lured a fourteen-year-old into prostitution served only 365 days in jail. Today, there are many advocates for stronger anti-trafficking laws and greater protection and assistance for survivors of all forms of human trafficking, but the problem continues to grow.

More than fifteen years ago, the US State Department began issuing a Trafficking in Persons Report, known as the TIP Report.[89] The TIP Report is used as the "principal diplomatic tool to engage foreign governments on human trafficking." The report attempts to monitor and rank countries' efforts to combat human trafficking and comply with international humanitarian law. While highly imperfect, as human trafficking mainly takes place hidden in the shadows and is hard to detect, with scores of cases going unreported to authorities, it is a significant step in the right direction.

Still, most agree it is not enough to end the evil of human trafficking.[90] It will take many more people of determination and conviction to stand against the tyranny of human trafficking and care for the most vulnerable among us. Only with a concerted, coordinated effort can and we hope to remove this modern-day scourge from our country and from the rest of the world.

The good news is that digital technology is providing another effective weapon in our arsenal to combat the plague of human trafficking and slavery. In the next two chapters, we will take a look at how some digital Davids are doing their part to take on the global Goliath of the sex-slave industries by using these technologies.

CHAPTER 17

THE HIGH-TECH WAR TO SAVE TRAFFICKED CHILDREN

It's an all too common scenario. A provocative photo of a twenty-year-old, taken in a nondescript hotel room, appears in an online escort services ad. The "twenty-year-old" is actually sixteen and was reported missing eight months ago.

Meanwhile, you're out of town on business, representing your company at a two-day industry conference. The conference is at a popular, higher-end hotel brand in a large city, which also gave attendees a nice discount on rooms.

At the end of a long day, you head up to your room, ready to go to bed and get up early the next day. But you're a light sleeper, so you can't help but notice the door across the hall keeps opening and shutting at odd hours during the night. There's no loud music or shouting, so there's no reason to complain; just a normal night in a busy hotel. You put it out of your mind and finally go to sleep.

You have no idea that the room across the hall is the room from the escort services ad, and sex trafficking is happening literally across the hall.

But even if you had suspected it, without clear evidence, what could you have done?

Luckily, there's an app for that.

TraffickCam, a joint project of the nonprofit Exchange Initiative, Washington University in St. Louis, and Temple University, allows users to upload pictures of their hotel room to a database that law enforcement can access to quickly identify the location of photos from escort ads.

Those online hotel room photos are often the best lead detectives have. They scour them for identifiable features such as pillows, paintings, and landmarks visible through the windows to identify the location or at least the hotel chain. But it can take weeks or months to sift through these ads and make a positive identification.

Now, instead of weeks or months, identification can take seconds. And tracking down traffickers—and rescuing children—just got a lot easier.

It all began when conference planners Molly Hackett, Jane Quinn, and Kimberly Ritter discovered sex trafficking was happening in their hometown of St. Louis, Missouri—and in hotels they knew well.

Hackett and Quinn are the co-founders of Nix Conference & Meeting Management in St. Louis, and Ritter is a director at Nix.

"In 2008, the Sisters of St. Joseph [in St. Louis] came to Nix and asked us to locate a hotel that would fight sex trafficking to use for their event," said Ritter. "That was the first we had heard of the issue, so we did some research."

They were shocked to discover that child sex trafficking was not only a first-world problem; it was a local problem. In fact, the FBI had listed St. Louis in the top twenty metropolitan areas in the United States for sex trafficking, likely because of its central location as a transportation hub.[91]

"Nix is a meeting planning company owned and operated by women with children ages twelve to fourteen years old, the average age of entry," explained Ritter. "We knew our own children were at risk. We also realized we had the professional resources to go to hotels and let them know this was happening."

"Because hotels are the primary location used by traffickers," added Hackett, "we soon realized that our travel industry expertise and connections could make a real difference for victims."

Immediately, Nix began educating the hotels where they did business—in seventeen countries and four continents—about the realities of sex trafficking, how to recognize it, and how to address and prevent it.

Fortunately, the anti-trafficking policy organization ECPAT-USA (part of ECPAT-International) offers robust resources for the private sector, especially the tourism industry.

Nix encouraged hotels to endorse the Tourism Child-Protection Code of Conduct ("the Code"), a joint venture between ECPAT-USA and the tourism industry. According to its website, the Code helps endorsers to:

1. Establish a policy and procedures against sexual exploitation of children.

2. Train employees in children's rights, the prevention of sexual exploitation, and how to report suspected cases.

3. Include a clause in contracts throughout the value chain stating a common repudiation and zero tolerance policy of sexual exploitation of children.

4. Provide information to travelers on children's rights, the prevention of sexual exploitation of children and how to report suspected cases.

5. Support, collaborate [with], and engage stakeholders in the prevention of sexual exploitation of children.

6. Report annually on their implementation of Code-related activities.[92]

"At that time, only hotels could sign the ECPAT Code of Conduct, but as meeting planners, we knew our industry was more of a powerhouse because we could effect change at the hotels we worked with," said Ritter.

So, Nix worked with ECPAT-Thailand to create the inaugural ECPAT-USA Meeting Planners Code of Conduct in January 2012 and was the first to sign it.

To consolidate their corporate responsibility efforts, they created the social action organization Exchange Initiative, where Hackett and Quinn are principal partners, and Ritter is Trafficking Initiative Coordinator.

The Exchange Initiative's first official task was, not surprisingly, to host a conference. IGNITE: Sparking Action Against Sex Trafficking brought together law enforcement, corporate executives, travel planners, community leaders, and educators to unite in the battle against sex trafficking.

"We felt the conference was the best way to bring all stakeholders together to educate them in one forum, so everyone could realize they all play a part in this," Ritter said. "As meeting planners, we were able to make an impact in sex trafficking, and every one of the stakeholders could, too."

What began as a sense of corporate responsibility became a mission. In Ritter's continuing research, she came upon Backpage.com, an online advertising site that includes an "escort services" section. The Nix colleagues soon discovered they could identify local hotel rooms in some of the photos advertising kids.

"Because of my personal connections to police officers, I reached out to local officers and let them know of rooms we identified in ads. I was even able to go on [our] first rescue," said Ritter.

"At that time, there was one officer in the St. Louis County Police Department, Sergeant Adam Kavanaugh, who worked on trafficking cases. He is still there, and now there are at least seven officers who work full-time to rescue children as part of the department's Human Trafficking and Child Predator Unit."

The local daily newspaper, the *St. Louis Post-Dispatch*, ran an article on their efforts to identify and rescue trafficking victims based on hotel room photos, and according to Ritter, many national media outlets, including CNN, picked up the story.

"After we received media attention, we started getting more photos to see if we could recognize," said Ritter. "A church group in Chicago I had connected with sent us a photo of a girl in desperate conditions, but we couldn't help because it was a smaller hotel we hadn't worked with. It was then that we started thinking of how we could get more hotel photos to help identify more victims' locations."

They also realized that every moment a child was held captive was a moment too many. "The first time we helped law enforcement locate a trafficked child, it took three days to locate that girl. We knew that was way too long," said Hackett.

Meanwhile, across town at Washington University in St. Louis, research associate Abby Stylianou was part of a team at the Media and Machines Lab that used computer vision techniques to identify where photographs were taken. They had already assisted the St. Louis Police Department in a cold case and were looking for more opportunities to use this technology for good.[93]

"Back in 2013, we consulted with the St. Louis Police Department to use computer vision to track down the location of a lost grave of a young crime victim, who in 1983 had been decapitated," Stylianou explained. "We were able ultimately to identify the location of her gravesite using computer vision techniques."[94]

Stylianou was then recruited to be part of the FBI Citizens Academy, where community leaders can learn more about the work of the FBI. The week they were discussing sex trafficking just happened to be the same week the *St. Louis Post-Dispatch* ran their story on three local women who were trying to crowdsource photos of hotel rooms to assist in trafficking investigations.[95]

Immediately, Stylianou thought, "I'd like to meet that lady, because I can help her."[96]

A meeting was set, and Exchange Initiative leadership met with Stylianou and her mentor, Dr. Robert Pless, professor of Computer Science and Engineering at Washington University.[97]

"They were using all sorts of super, high-level coordinates of random photos taken outside and showing how they could find their original locations," said Hackett. "They said they could probably do this with interiors. While they're doing this, I'm touching my phone. And I asked them, can you make an app for us?"[98]

The result was TraffickCam, which is composed of two parts. The first is the free app available to the public, where anyone can upload photos of their hotel room to a central database.

From a user experience, the app couldn't be easier: "You just enter your hotel room and your room number. You take four pictures, and you submit them to the website," said Stylianou.[99]

To prevent manipulation of the data, GPS location is used to verify the user's location. "No other personal data is captured," said Hackett.

Advanced computer imaging techniques take care of the rest. Those photos become part of an enormous database of images that law enforcement officials can access, which is the second part of TraffickCam.

To most people, standard hotel rooms look pretty similar. Not to the application created by the team at Washington and Temple Universities. Any one picture has thousands of data points, which their image analysis technology can identify and catalog.

When law enforcement uploads photos of possible minors from escort ads to the TraffickCam database, "the search algorithms will run and return to the investigators the most probable location of those victims," she said.[100]

"Criminals take advantage of technology to advertise and coordinate illegal sex trafficking," said Pless. "We're using new technologies to fight sex trafficking, with this app that allows everyone to contribute data and with new image analysis tools to help law enforcement use the images in investigations."[101]

The free app for Apple and Android was released in 2016.

"When TraffickCam launched, news of the app truly went viral," said Hackett. "We tracked more than 5,000 news stories in the first few months. In just the first month of Twitter activity, we saw tweets from almost every country!"

According to the Exchange Initiative's latest data, TraffickCam has been downloaded 152,000 times and receives an average of 212 submissions per *day*. More than 257,000 hotels are represented in the database, with nearly three million images.

Although the Exchange Initiative and law enforcement can't share specific stories about rescued children due to confidentiality, they are enthusiastic about the app's potential, especially in providing tangible evidence that can lead to more effective prosecutions.

"The app created by the Exchange Initiative will give law enforcement yet another technological tool to reach that goal in a quicker, more proficient manner when investigating cases involving human trafficking and child exploitation," said Kavanaugh. [102]

Of course, just because officials are able to identify the hotel room from a photo, it doesn't mean the traffickers are currently at that location. Traffickers often use multiple strategies with their victims. For example, when speaking to CNN, Ritter explained that "traffickers often post photographs from one location to advertise services in another." Or they may be based in a central location and transport the children to the areas that respond.[103]

However, even in these cases, evidence from the app can be used to create a sting operation, or build an effective case against traffickers that work across state lines.

"We can then make a federal case because of the interstate commerce," said Kavanaugh to CNN.[104] Providing clear evidence of where traffickers have been over time helps with prosecution and stronger sentencing.[105]

"The response to TraffickCam and the issue of human trafficking is a huge success story," said Hackett. "Millions have learned of the issue of sex trafficking through news articles and social media posts about TraffickCam. Tens of thousands have taken direct action by uploading images to TraffickCam and sharing articles and posts about the issue. We have been contacted by all major law enforcement in the United States and many internationally."

The Sisters of St. Joseph, the group who first alerted the Nix colleagues about sex trafficking, continue to support their mission. "The app would not be possible without funding from the congregation of the Sisters of St. Joseph," said Hackett. "Thanks to their generous matching gift, every dollar given to Exchange Initiative is doubled, up to $100,000, to help eradicate sex trafficking."

With TraffickCam, private citizens around the world can instantly assist in an active investigation, and even prevent trafficking before it starts.

"Child trafficking is hard to look at," said Hackett, "but TraffickCam has broadened awareness and empowered everyone to do something to make a difference."

The Polaris Project, named after the North Star that guided fugitive slaves north on the Underground Railroad, is another example of an anti-trafficking group that is making full use of digital media to help guide victims to freedom.

For example, out of recognition that trafficking is often a trans-national crime—while most law enforcement is limited by national borders—the Polaris Project helped to create an innovative informa-tion sharing network that increases the ability of local law enforcement agencies to share data and collaborate in freeing victims. In the case of human trafficking across the US-Mexico border—a huge problem in the southern United States—Polaris has played a leading role in helping to network American and Mexican law enforcement as well as trafficking victim support organizations and hotlines. As a result, both Americans and Mexicans are better protected from traffickers than they would be in the absence of such sophisticated tools.

In addition, Polaris has created an online Global Modern Slavery Directory that connects victims and those at-risk for victimization with anti-trafficking organizations and resources. While this may seem like an obvious remedy, the reality is that most local anti-trafficking groups lack the resources and sophistication to create such resources themselves while also doing the frontline work of rescuing, sheltering, counselling, and protecting those vulnerable to trafficking. That is where Polaris and their digital savvy comes in.

CHAPTER 18

A WAY OUT 4 WOMEN FROM MODERN SLAVERY

Atlanta is fast becoming known as the sex trafficking capital of America. According to a study by the Urban Institute for the National Institute of Justice, Atlanta generated more revenue from the sex industry than any other major American city they surveyed. Escorts can make $1,000 an hour, and pimps can make nearly $33,000 a week. Why Atlanta? The authors of the study theorize that the high number of conventions and events in the area is the cause.[106] Others point to the fact that traffickers generally prefer busy airports—with Atlanta being America's busiest.

Regardless of the reason, the lucrative sex industry comes at a high cost for the women involved—who are often just teenagers when they enter "the life," as many prostituted women call it. Too many end up feeling trapped—and end up abused, addicted, or dead.

Melissa was one of these women. She was raised by her father in Atlanta, who passed away suddenly when she was fifteen. Rather than face the foster care system, she ran away from home and ended up on the street. She was introduced to "the life" by the very first man she met, and she did not look back.

By the time Melissa was twenty, she had a pimp and a regular ad on Backpage.com, which brought her regular customers. One day, she received a strange call on her cell phone.

"Hi," the woman said. "I want to let you know that I'm not with law enforcement. I'm with an organization called '4Sarah,' and we help women in the sex industry. We want to text you our hotline number in case you're ever in a bad situation, a crisis, and you need somewhere safe to go or if you ever want to get out of 'the life.' Do you mind if I text you our hotline number?"

Melissa didn't see how that could hurt, so she said, "Yeah, okay." A few seconds after she hung up, a phone number came through from 4Sarah. She did not call the number, but she did not delete it, either.

Every once in a while, she would get a new text from 4Sarah, making sure she was okay and letting her know that if she ever needed help, she could contact them any time, day or night. She thought about that number when her pimp started to beat her and would not allow her to take showers. But she was not ready to leave the life. It was all she had ever known. How could she make a living any other way?

A few months later, a window of unexpected freedom opened. Her pimp had a heart attack and ended up in the hospital. Melissa remembered that phone number. She dialed it and simply said, "I'm ready now." And that was all Kasey McClure, founder of 4Sarah, needed to hear.

"I took her to the bus station the next day to get her somewhere safe, and we got her out of the state of Georgia into a program that can take individual girls immediately," said McClure. Melissa is in one of those programs now. "She walked away from that life, and it was due to her ad being posted on Backpage that we were able to reach out to her."

McClure knows exactly what it's like to be a woman employed in the sex industry, and how hard it is to walk away. "My dad molested me from the time I was three years old, and a couple others too. Then I became sexually active at a young age, and to me, the sex industry was a way for me to get out of poverty and get on my own," she said.

"I left home and started stripping at eighteen. My sister started stripping at seventeen. A lot of girls go into this thinking that it's going to create a better life than what they have now, but they don't realize that it gets you trapped and in bondage for the rest of your life. Some of the girls—especially the girls that are escorting and prostituting on the streets or online—they're at risk of getting HIV. They're also at high risk of getting killed."

After six years in the industry, and after getting married, McClure finally found the courage to leave. But she also soon found herself over $60,000 in debt—and sorely tempted to return to stripping, where she made over $1,000 a night. Her turning point was becoming pregnant with her daughter, Sarah. That's when she knew, for the sake of her daughter, she could never go back. In 2005, she founded her nonprofit, 4Sarah, to help women like herself leave "the life" and support them with resources so they would never be tempted to return again—not just for their own sake but for the sake of their daughters and other girls who look up to them.

McClure and her team reach out to girls and women in the sex industry, both online and offline. In addition to randomly calling the phone numbers from online escort ads, as they did with Melissa, they also visit Atlanta-area strip clubs to connect with girls and women personally. For those who contact them, 4Sarah connects them to a program that offers them safety and support. The organization partners with a number of live-in centers geared toward helping girls and women involved in the sex industry get the education, training, counseling, and support they need to create a new life.

4Sarah also offers a $2,500 educational scholarship every three months to girls and women who are in the life, coming out of the life, or in a program, based on an essay submission. Most of their submissions come from around the country via the internet and a Google search on terms such as "sex industry scholarship."

McClure and her team first began their online outreach in 2007 by calling girls and women listed under the escort section on Craigslist. After Craigslist decided to shut down their escort section, when some murders were linked to their listings, 4Sarah then focused on the escort listings on Backpage.

"You never really know what you're going to get," says McClure. "When you click on the ad, it'll be a description of what they offer. They try to get your interest because they want you to call, of course. When they provide a phone number…sometimes it's their real cell phone number, and sometimes it's a Google Voice phone number. They can create a fake phone number through Google, and because they can't use their real cell phones, it protects them a little bit."

4Sarah outreach workers simply call the phone number listed with the ad and let women know they are there to help whenever they need it, texting them the hotline number if they give them permission. "Most of the time they respond," McClure says. "They're very nice. Sometimes they're not interested, but our main focus is to give them our hotline number and our website. What they do with it, we don't always know."

For example, one woman decided to pass the information on to a friend before contacting 4Sarah for herself. "We met her through Backpage," says McClure. "She wasn't ready to get out of the life at the time, but she had a friend that she wanted us to help who was working on Backpage as well. We connected with her friend and got her into a program. She was in the program for fourteen months and did extremely well. This woman had been in the life for twenty-three years, and she got out.

"Eventually this young lady we were calling also got out of the life. She had been beaten and punched in the mouth for years throughout her being on the streets, and we were able to connect her with a dentist who provided free dentures for her. She also became a scholarship recipient to go to a training course for leadership, and she's also doing really well."

Even when they don't ask for help directly, McClure has found that many women they contact are very willing to share their stories. "I've heard stories that are pretty sad. For example, some girls start prostituting at eighteen. They meet a guy who introduces them to that world, and he tells them, 'I know how you can make some extra money, and I'll protect you,' and he ends up pimping them out and beating them.

"Some girls come to Georgia thinking they're going to be in a movie or work for a casting agency, and they end up getting connected with a pimp. One lady we talked to through Backpage even told us about a pimp who pulled up to three girls standing on a corner. He asked all three of them who had a pimp. When one of the girls said that she didn't, he snatched her and threw her in the trunk of his car."

Since McClure and her team visit Atlanta's strip clubs and red-light districts regularly, they often come face to face with several pimps who are none too happy to see them.

"Yeah, we do piss a few off," McClure says, laughing. "We've got a couple in jail who are mad at us right now, but they'll be okay. They'll get over it."

4Sarah has also taken advantage of Backpage's willingness to share information with law enforcement when minors may be involved. In January 2015, an Atlanta city commissioner decided he wanted to educate lawmakers about sex trafficking in Atlanta, and he contacted McClure to ask her if she could take a group of them on a bus tour and show them the hot spots.

Over thirty people went on that bus tour—including Atlanta's local news crew from Channel 2. When the story aired that night, a worried grandmother was watching. Her fourteen-year-old granddaughter had been missing for over a month, and her family was beginning to fear she had run away and been enticed into prostitution. Luckily, they publicized 4Sarah's twenty-four-hour hotline number, and the grandmother called it that night. "I have a fourteen-year-old granddaughter who I think might be in sex trafficking," she said. "Can you help us?"

Her granddaughter had been listed as missing and exploited, and she had begun using a new nickname all of a sudden, shortly before she had run away. "[The grandmother] gave us her nickname and her description, and she sent us some pictures we could use," said McClure.

The hotline volunteer immediately called Ann Bailey, 4Sarah's intervention coordinator, with this information. Bailey happened to be with McClure on the way home to Atlanta from Kentucky, where they had been visiting some women from one of their partner programs. "As we were driving back, Ann used her cell phone and pulled up Backpage, searching on some of the characteristics, and we used that nickname in the search on the website. That was the first ad that popped up. That little girl used her nickname. In a matter of thirty minutes, with the description she gave us, we were able to locate this child on Backpage."

McClure sent that ad and the girl's description to Internet Crimes against Children (ICAC), a national network of sixty-one coordinated task forces created to help law enforcement respond effectively to internet-based crimes against children. "They were able to track that ad to the person who listed that ad through Backpage to the address of where this credit card was used, which was where they were living," explained McClure. "And they did a sting operation, went in, and busted the guy. The girl was not there at the time, but he gave them information, and they were able to not only locate that child, but also locate another fifteen-year-old girl who was about to go on her first call.

"It was incredible. Law enforcement, everybody, came together perfectly, like a circle."

It turned out the fourteen-year-old girl had run away, but she had also been recruited by some other girls and got connected with the pimp. "Sometimes these little girls want to get out and grow up too fast, and she was one of them, trying to grow up too fast, and she got herself in trouble," said McClure.

McClure is quick to point out both the positives and negatives of Backpage.com as a sex industry commerce site. One positive she notes, "If you see anything that does not look right, you can report that to Backpage and they will work with the National Center for Missing and Exploited Children and investigate it. So, it's a tool for law enforcement to look for people, particularly for missing kids.

McClure is also quick to mention the good that 4Sarah has been able to do through digital technology and how it can empower many others as well. "I think definitely those girls are changing their lives because we located them online."

Backpage Shut Down

Although Backpage.com had cooperated with law enforcement and anti-trafficking groups, the public furor over their adult and escort classified section ultimately produced the political conditions for the website's demise. On April 6, 2018, the Federal Bureau of Investigation seized Backpage.com and affiliated websites and shut them down. Owners, executives, and employees were also arrested."[107]

Shortly thereafter, Backpage.com's CEO Carl Ferrer pleaded guilty to conspiracy, money laundering, and facilitating prostitution after he admitted that "he had long been aware that the great majority of Backpage's 'escort' and 'adult' advertisements are, in fact, advertisements for prostitution services."

"For far too long, Backpage.com existed as the dominant marketplace for illicit commercial sex, a place where sex traffickers frequently advertised children and adults alike," former US Attorney General Jeff Sessions said in a statement. "But this illegality stops right now… it can no longer be used by criminals to promote and facilitate human trafficking."[108]

As technology and the expansive growth of the internet have obviated laws intended to keep women and children safe from human traffickers, the need for new legislation has become apparent. In response, the United States Congress, in a bipartisan effort, passed legislation to fight online sex trafficking and hold websites liable for hosting trafficking content. Congress enacted the "Allow States and Victims to Fight Online Sex Trafficking Act," also known as FOSTA.

According to Speaker of the House of Representatives Paul Ryan's Press Office, "In addition to making it easier for states to investigate and prosecute businesses that facilitate online sex trafficking, FOSTA equips states with more effective tools to do so. And it empowers victims to seek justice by providing recourse for them to sue."[109]

So, the good news is, as a result of FOSTA, law enforcement finally has the tools they need to hold websites accountable for engaging and profiting from sex trafficking while also providing a pathway for victims to "sue internet companies they accuse of hosting content that facilitated sex trafficking."[110]

Already prominent websites, like Craigslist and Reddit, reacted to FOSTA by moving swiftly to bring their digital platforms in full compliance. They removed potential infringing personal ad sections from their websites. As such, these digital platforms are doing their part to help keep the internet a safe place that is free from human and child trafficking.

For McClure and groups like 4Sarah and Exchange Initiative, the ongoing battle to combat the heinous crime of sex trafficking is everyone's responsibility. By being watchful, remaining informed and sharing the good work of these groups with our own network, we can help to raise awareness of their work and the resources they offer. Working together, we have more power to combat this plague on society and our children.

CHAPTER 19

OPPORTUNITY IN EMERGING MARKETS

Equality of economic opportunity is another important principle enshrined in the Universal Declaration of Human Rights because of its ability to unleash human potential and promote economic and social flourishing. Unfortunately, in many parts of the world, this freedom is denied to some members of society—with social, cultural, and religious barriers putting women at a particular disadvantage in many emerging market economies.

Although governments and international agencies have long sought to address this intransigent problem, one encouraging feature of our age has been a trend toward entrepreneurs employing digital technology in ways that allow formerly disenfranchised groups to participate in local economies. One notable example of this trend is the rise of "mobile money" services for those who do not have access to traditional banking or financial institutions.[111]

Travelers Cheques, credit cards, and debit cards are all financial inventions that have revolutionized commerce and made banking and other financial services easier and more convenient for people around the world. The concept of mobile money, also sometimes referred to as e-wallets, may be the next emerging revolution to help bring financial freedom and access to more people by enabling them to pay bills and transfer and receive money online using their cell phones. In some parts of the world, individuals use mobile money as an additional financial tool *with* cash while others use it *instead of* cash.

Having access to reliable and secure financial services is a critical component to ending poverty, especially in places where there are no banks or financial services infrastructure.

The growing number of people with cell phones has made mobile money accessible to large sectors of society—including many formerly-disenfranchised groups in the developing world. There are several major companies globally who provide mobile money services.

Other companies like the London-based WorldRemit are also offering mobile money services as an option to transfer money abroad inexpensively.[112] While studying in London, founder and Somali entrepreneur Ismail Ahmed frequently needed to send funds to his family members back home in Africa. The costs and fees were enormous. As WorldRemit's vision states, "We live in a world of instant global communications. Yet the business of sending money abroad has remained stuck in the past."

By optimizing the services of mobile money, individuals using WorldRemit now have a less-expensive alternative to traditional banking to transfer money abroad to fifty countries.

A United Nations whistleblower who exposed corruption, Ahmed has taken his experience and parlayed it in the private sector.[113] Recently, WorldRemit secured funding from investors behind successful digital media companies including Facebook, Dropbox, and Spotify to expand its reach and digital financial services.[114]

Now let's take a closer look at how mobile money is helping and empowering women in Chad.

Consider the story of Nya. She is the president of the Chadian Fish Seller's Association in Ngara, near Lake Chad. The economics of selling fish in Chad is relatively straightforward: Each morning, Nya and her fellow fish sellers take their proceeds from yesterday's sales, walk to the lake, and trade with the fisherman to buy fish to sell at the market that day. When fish sellers show up at the lake with money, the fishermen know they can't leave until they've bought something, so it's often difficult to get a good price. Once they negotiate a price, they buy their fish and then have to pay someone to drive it up to the market, where they'll sell it and hopefully also make a profit. The next day, they'll take their proceeds back to the lake and bargain again, same as before.

The problem is that the fish-selling industry in Chad, like its society in general, is very male-dominated. Women have a notoriously hard time not only negotiating prices with the fisherman, but also selling at a fair price in the market. So it can be very hard to earn a living.

But when mobile money came to her area, it transformed the way Nya did business, according to Greg Reeve, a digital entrepreneur and General Manager of Millicom Mobile Financial Services, one global mobile money provider. Reeve spoke with Nya personally during his travels to her community. "Now they phone ahead to the lake and say, 'Well, I'm thinking of buying. Maybe I will, maybe I won't, but what sort of deals have you got?'" he explains. "Suddenly, you're not there with the cash, and the prices are maybe a bit better, because you can phone someone else and you can get a good price. It's simple market economics."

When Nya and the fisherman agree on a price, she simply asks him to ship it by truck to her at her market stall, and she'll pay him to cover the fish and the shipping. When the fish arrives, she can instantly send the money to the fisherman through her mobile phone—which saves her the time and effort of physically going down to the lake and hiring a truck herself. As a result, she can negotiate a better buying price and thus increase her profit.

"That means that suddenly, they're in charge of the economics of the situation," says Reeve. "They buy and sell their fish at a better price. Certainly, they're a bit more powerful in the market."

But what really drove the point home for Reeve was what Nya said next.

"She sort of leaned forward, and she said, 'In fact, we've actually negotiated with the market owners and they're going to be creating a new latrine. At the moment, there's only one latrine, and it's a male one. We share it, but now they're going to build a new one just for us women.' I thought, *That is power!* That's what made me realize we've elevated them from one normal trader to a more organized group," Reeve says.

"That is an example of women understanding the technology and using it to be able to empower themselves in business, which has not only enriched them in terms of money, but in terms of status in the market to the point where they're actually speaking with a more conjoined voice and actually getting more things done for themselves. If you haven't got that, then they'd be back at square one, walking to the fish sellers beside the lake early in the morning to try to buy fish at a bad rate. Again, mobile money—it does allow people who understand it to change the economics of day-to-day transactions."

Many emerging markets have cultural practices that keep women from taking virtually any action without their husband's permission. But mobile money allows women to open accounts independently from their husbands, often for the first time. With mobile money providers such as Vodafone and Millicom, a woman can open a free mobile money account, no questions asked, and deposit money into it herself. And that information is kept private, even from her husband. Now she has the opportunity to protect some money of her own to further support her family and perhaps even save enough to get ahead of her daily expenses.

"Typically, women make better use of money in a family situation than men, helping to ensure that funds go to food, medicines and other items to help the family," explains Reeve. In an environment where cash can be the enemy of poor people, especially women, mobile money has transformed cash into economic power.

As important as financially empowering women is, it's truly just the tip of the iceberg. In a variety of ways, mobile money is financially empowering the largest market sector in emerging markets—the poor majority.

"Banks don't really address the needs of customers who are what we'd call the 'bottom of the pyramid,'" says Reeve. "Primarily, it's because they're expensive to manage and difficult to reach." And these customers often feel the same way about the banks: the fees to open an account, maintain an account, transfer money, and pay the inevitable penalty fee for dropping below a minimum balance can add up to be more than they would need to live each day. Beyond the banks, conventional money-transfer services such as Western Union, which typically cost 12 percent of the amount sent per transaction, are no more affordable.

In contrast, mobile money customers pay nothing to open an account, maintain an account, or deposit money into the account. Transferring money costs 1 to 1.5 percent and removing money from the account costs 2 percent. Now the vast majority of people in emerging markets have access to the same level of convenience and protection banks offer their customers, introducing them to a whole new level of financial empowerment.

In fact, mobile money offers a variety of sophisticated financial services to the underserved poor. In Tanzania, Millicom pays its customers interest on the money they keep on their phone, just like a standard interest-bearing checking or savings account. Every quarter, Millicom customers receive a text message that alerts them they have new money in their account—a return on the funds they have kept in their account. But Millicom doesn't pay the rock-bottom rates a middle-class individual might earn on their checking or savings account at the local bank. It pays its customers around 9.5 percent annually—the same rate an account with millions of dollars in it would earn.

"Our e-money systems are based on the fact that for each cent of e-money we create, we hold the exact same amount in local banks in local currency. We take the interest on the real money that we hold in the bank and we just share it equally amongst the customers, based on how much money they have in their account," says Reeve. Because they keep all the small amounts of money they receive from customers in a single account, that multi-million dollar account earns the best interest rate from banks. And Millicom passes that same interest rate to all its customers, not just the ones who store the most money on their phones.

Mobile money has finally brought the power of compound interest to the poorest of the poor, often for the first time.

"We had one person call one of our agents from one of these mom-and-pop shops," says Reeve. "Basically, this guy was crying on the phone. He said, 'I've just got this money. I didn't realize it would be so much.' The interest was like almost getting a month's salary for him. He said, 'I've never heard of anyone ever sharing their profits before.' We said, 'We think this is the right thing to do. We think you're going to use the system more.' He said, 'Don't worry.'

"Another person was very grateful and said, 'I didn't know money could grow.' That was the major breakthrough. We explained, 'Your money's growing, so we're giving you the growth.' That's what everyone's doing with money. All this is about education—explaining to people what they can do. Once they get it, that's it. They've now got a new way of doing things that they never had before."

And once people begin growing their money, they now have money to save. Of course, the concept of saving isn't new; in Ghana, those who manage to accumulate some extra money typically use a system called Susu. If you have money you want to keep safe from theft or impending flood, or just for unexpected emergencies, you give it to the "Susu man" for safekeeping.

When you need your money, you'll need to find the Susu man (wherever he may be) and ask for your money back. Then he'll give you your money, minus a 5 to 6 percent service charge. The problem is knowing whether the Susu man is trustworthy; many have been known to keep money safe for a while, but once they've accumulated a lot of money, they could disappear. Saving money can be very costly indeed.

As an alternative, Millicom has a service called the "digital Susu," which provides the same level of convenience and security as a bank's savings account, but it operates the way people in Ghana would expect— except now they never have to wonder when the Susu man will come back to their village or if he's trustworthy. They can deposit their money on their phone, it remains safe, and when they need it, they can withdraw it minus a 2 percent service charge, lower than what the Susu man would charge.

"Because they trust us and because we don't run off with their money, the money is always there. Digital Susu is an excellent way of keeping your money safe, and a lot of people use it."[115]

As customers continue to grow their money through the power of compound interest and begin saving that money, they also begin to think about further protecting themselves against emergencies and the inevitable cash flow problems that come from barely having enough to live on.

"If you're earning two dollars a day and you are suddenly sick, you're not earning two dollars a day," says Reeve. "But if you've got enough money from the extra ten cents that you made because you were able to use the system every day to send money, so you get an extra ten cents a day, over a month you've probably got enough to say, 'You know what? I've got enough to buy some insurance now. If I get sick, it's going to be okay for me and my family, because it will cover me for the period of sickness.'"

So Millicom also offers micro-insurance—small, affordable policy packages that cost the equivalent of US $1.50 a month and cover life insurance, permanent disability, and emergency hospitalization or maternity coverage. Mobile money customers can pay for that insurance directly from their mobile phone or even via air time, since most people have prepaid accounts. Millicom's micro-insurance provider is selling 700,000 new policies a month, and those numbers are increasing.

Life insurance is particularly helpful in cultures where funerals are elaborate, expensive, multi-day affairs, such as in Ghana. "When you die, your family, your tribe, and the people you know all want to bury you, and they'll all need to come. If they're in different parts of the country, you have to organize that, so they're all there at the same time," explains Reeve.

In addition to the vast numbers of attendees and multiday social events, there's the burdensome cost of the coffin. In Ghana, an individual is buried in an elaborate coffin that represents what that person did for a living or what he or she was known for. A fisherman would be buried in a coffin shaped like a fish, a car salesman in a car, and so on. If you Google "Ghana coffins," you'll see many more examples.

"People save up money for funerals," says Reeve. "Culturally, it's really important." These are the same people who live on barely two US dollars a day, so the economic burden of this cultural tradition is obvious. But life insurance allows people to use the money they would have saved for funerals on expenses that could make their lives easier *before* their funeral as well.

All technology is subject to abuse—and mobile money is no exception. But most experts agree that the good this digital tool has accomplished outweighs its potential for harm. Women are able to save money to protect their families. The underserved poor now have access to the power of compound interest and are able to get ahead of their daily expenses for perhaps the first time in their lives. Economic power bases are shifting for the better and becoming more inclusive. Previously marginalized people are not just protecting their money, but growing it— providing a foundation of personal wealth and security that can improve the lives of many generations to come.

CHAPTER 20

THE CLOUD CAN ALSO SAVE FOOD

What do you do when you see that grocery stores and bakeries are throwing out perfectly good food, while down the street, charities are raising money to buy food?

If you are in Ireland or the United Kingdom—thanks to two digital Good Samaritans—you can use an app to do something about it.

What began in Dublin as an idea and a shared passion at Trinity College between two women—Iseult Ward, a law and accounting graduate, and Aoibheann O'Brien, a business major—has become a digital movement to combat hunger and food waste.

Introducing: FoodCloud, a nonprofit social enterprise that is another tribute to the potential of the Digital Age.

As co-founder Ward explains, "The concept was simple. Match the business with too much food with local charities and community groups which have too little, through the use of a smartphone app."[116]

Among other things, the FoodCloud story illustrates that *Human Liberty 2.0* is not simply for geeks. Although neither O'Brien nor Ward is particularly tech savvy, the enterprising women were able to have an app developed to realize their vision. "Imagine a world where no food goes to waste," says Ward. "That is the world that we want to live in."

How do they do it? "It's about the business and charities working together in a practical way to make their communities better—and that trickles down to making the whole society better," says Ward. "It is a win-win for both sides of the equation. By redistributing food at a local level, businesses no longer have to pay to dispose of perfectly good food when they can donate it. At the same time, they are contributing to their community in a meaningful and practical way to combat both food waste and food poverty. For the charities receiving the donated food, not only can they provide healthy meals for those in need, they are able to redirect resources which otherwise would have gone to food to other needs."[117]

Every day, businesses, grocery stores, and bakeries who are part of FoodCloud upload a description of the surplus and unsold food that they wish to donate through their smart phones or computers via FoodCloud's app. Next, the FoodCloud app alerts charities via text message regarding the type and amount of surplus food that is available. If the charity or community group is not in need, they do not accept, and the offer goes to another charity, but if they are in need, they click "accept." From there, arrangements for pick-up are made at no charge to the charity or community group. The businesses pay an annual subscription fee to be a part of FoodCloud, which costs less than what they were spending to dispose of perfectly good food.

"One in eight people in Ireland experience food poverty," while "1 million tonnes of food" was being thrown out by Irish consumers and businesses every year. This is a global problem. "One in seven people experiences food poverty worldwide."[118] Meanwhile, almost 30 percent of the food that is produced globally is wasted.

Moreover, there is a moral dimension to the coexistence of hunger and food waste in modern societies. With such an excess of available food, no one should ever go hungry in a free and developed society, but they do.

After years of seeing a decline in global hunger, starvation, malnutrition, and undernourishment, World Health Organization (WHO) has found this positive trend reversing. According to WHO key global findings for 2018:

- 462 million adults globally are underweight.
- 52 million children under five years of age malnourished and underweight.
- Around 45 percent of deaths among children under five years of age are linked to lack of proper nutrition.[119]

The good news is thanks to innovative app creators like FoodCloud and other start-ups, who are all using the power of digital and social media, food redistribution can play a crucial role in eradicating hunger and food waste.

FoodCloud, like most good ideas, initially started small. Ward and O'Brien began by approaching a single grocery store chain, Tesco Ireland, which liked their idea and disliked having to pay to dispose of perfectly good food every day. So, they agreed to test the FoodCloud concept at one store location. The pilot project was so successful that over time they expanded until FoodCloud was available for all of Tesco Ireland's stores—over 120 locations!

But as FoodCloud grew there were also challenges, risks, and obstacles the co-founders had to overcome. Issues ranged from transportation to food storage to food safety.

Every country has its own food safety regulations and best practices. So, for the charities and businesses to be able to use FoodCloud, they must first sign an agreement to verify food safety compliance. FoodCloud also reserves the right to refuse any food that it considers unfit for consumption.

In a 2014 *TIME* magazine interview, as a part of the "Next Generation Leaders" series, Ward and O'Brien candidly spoke about the initial startup challenges and growing pains.

"The big break was when Iseult graduated and she applied for [LaunchBox]," says O'Brien, referring to a start-up accelerator

program. "Everything changed when we had that full-time power behind it." LaunchBox offered office space, business mentorship and a salary, which meant Ward had time to cold-call businesses, to research Ireland's charity industry, and to streamline donations by having an app built.

Moreover, as Ward would go on to explain, "Managing relationships with charities isn't part of a retailer's core business, so we had to make it really easy for them to donate food. Charities, on the other hand, are often understaffed and low on resources, so we had to make the process easy for them as well."[120]

Today, FoodCloud has several warehouses to store food for redistribution throughout Ireland and the United Kingdom. In 2017, less than five years after it first started, FoodCloud had crossed a remarkable milestone. Together with their FoodCloud hubs in Ireland and the UK, FoodCloud has redistributed twenty million meals through their vast network of local charities and community groups.[121]

As FoodCloud likes to say, surplus food should "feed people, not landfills."

CHAPTER 21

NEW YORKERS ARE
HUMAN AFTER ALL

As a native New Yorker, I feel a special pride in telling Brandon Stanton's remarkable story—a story that is deeply entwined with the amazing human mosaic of my hometown.

In 2010, like millions of Americans reeling from the global economic recession, Brandon Stanton was unemployed. A self-described "dreamer" originally from the Atlanta suburbs, Stanton had recently been fired from his job as a stock trader in Chicago. He had gone from making a lucrative living to being broke.[122]

The markets are "really just a bunch of people arguing over what something's worth, which is based on psychology," Stanton would later describe his time as a stock trader. The greed and fear that drives the markets had given him a glimpse into the raw side of human existence. After losing his job, Stanton wanted to do something different. He wanted to explore the human experience from an artistic angle. So, he started taking photographs, despite having no prior experience or training.[123]

Quickly, he became obsessed with his new calling. Stanton left Chicago for New Orleans, Philadelphia, Pittsburgh, and finally settled in New York, taking photographs all the way. He started photographing graffiti, architecture, nature, and then strangers, and posting a photoblog on Facebook, Twitter, Tumblr, and Instagram.

With the little money he had left, Stanton paid the down payment for a lease on an apartment in the Bedford-Stuyvesant neighborhood of Brooklyn. With his Canon EOS 7D camera, he decided to photograph 10,000 people in all five boroughs of New York City to create an interactive "digital map" that would act as a "photographic census" of the city. It was ambitious, but would it be possible for a struggling, neophyte photographer?[124]

In an interview, with the *Tim Ferriss Show*, Stanton recalled:

I was too addicted to taking photos to ever stop for a second and learn about photography. I have one memory of going to Barnes & Noble one night and flipping through some photography books and enjoying the photos—because I couldn't afford to buy any books. But I really wanted to be out taking pictures. I didn't really want to be studying how to take a correct photo. I just wanted to be out photographing. It was the act of it, the act of discovery. And I had a very amateur view of photography at the time, where if you get something or somebody interesting in the frame, it's a great photo. I don't care how many points perspective it has. I don't care about the rules of thirds. I honestly don't really even care about white balance or focus or any of these things. I was just looking for wonderful people and wonderful moments that were happening.[125]

With no fans, no money, and nobody paying attention to his photoblog, his family and friends back home thought he was crazy. He had gone from working as a well-paid stock trader to a low-income, untrained photographer running a blog that generated little income. His diet consisted of eggs and peanut butter-and-jelly sandwiches.[126]

For six months, he kept at it, asking scores of people if he could take their picture.

At over six feet tall with a high-pitched voice, many New Yorkers he approached balked at his request. They assumed he was some kind of a creep so "[insert vulgarity] off, loser," and variations thereof became a familiar response. For months, he was yelled at or ignored over and over again. He quickly learned to never approach people on the streets of New York from behind. [127]

Unknown to him at the time, Stanton was heading down a path to a career that would ultimately capture this fascinating digital moment we are all living in.

His fortunes changed after he photographed a woman with green hair, green makeup, wearing all green clothing, including green gloves.

Stanton remembered something she said when he asked her if he could take her picture. He asked, "So do you do a different color every day?" and she replied, "No, I used to go through different stages. But then I found that I was happiest when I was green, so I've been green for fifteen years."

Later that day he posted her photo on Facebook and used their exchange as the caption. To his surprise, he quickly got sixty-seven "likes." It was the most engaged photo he had ever taken. It was at that movement when Humans of New York was born. Stanton dumped his original plan to create a sweeping digital map of the city and decided instead to focus on individuals and their stories. [128]

For months, Stanton had been tinkering with the correct words to say when he approached people, having been rejected so many times. He would play with different approaches and words, such as "picture" versus "photograph"—every combination imaginable. Then he realized it had nothing to do with the words he was saying; it was about the energy he was giving off. If you walk up to someone and you are nervous, obviously they are going to become nervous, too, and wonder what was going on. He would begin with, "Do you mind if I take your photograph?" and then he'd quickly start asking questions about them, such as, "What is your greatest struggle right now?"

While many people are uncomfortable being publicly photographed, at the same time, they have a human desire to be heard. Stanton wanted to hear their stories. He actually cares about the stories of the people whose pictures he takes and wanted to know more.

Stanton had been mastering the ability to put people he had just met at ease while he was capturing photographs. He developed an ability to do this with people from all walks of life—different social backgrounds, ages, countries, ethnic groups, you name it.

Some of the stories he captures can be light and humorous. Others can be heartbreaking. Stanton has photographed survivors of child abuse; alcoholics trying to sober up; veterans suffering from PTSD; parents who admitted that they did not love their children as much as they thought they would.

Stanton's authentic ability to draw out raw, unfiltered, honest moments of people's personal stories while taking their picture made Humans of New York so popular that he now has more fans online than there are residents of New York City. Apparently, the world is paying attention!

From Photoblog to Philanthropy

In October 2012, a deadly hurricane named Sandy took Humans of New York from a photoblog to a philanthropic organization. Sandy had torn through the Caribbean and up the Atlantic coast, gaining power and strength. With hurricane winds at 175 miles from its eye, Sandy deluged fifteen states and killed about 150 people over the span of two weeks.

The storm rocked New York. It hit parts of New York City with such violent winds, that the floodwater poured incongruously like waterfalls off a mountainside into the New York City subway stations. On the evening of October 29, a storm surge fourteen feet high battered Battery Park in Manhattan. New York Harbor was hit with waves of up to thirty-three feet high.[129]

In Breezy Point, the tip of the Rockaway Peninsula in Queens, rising seawater came in contact with electrical wires, and a house caught on fire. Winds from Sandy spread flames and it became an inferno. More than 200 homes burned to the ground in the city that night—one hundred twenty-six in the Rockaway community alone.[130] Three nuclear reactors were shut down—two in New York and one in New Jersey.[131] At one point 7.9 million households and businesses in fifteen states were without electrical power.

Gasoline shortages spread, schools were closed, and some residents were forced to flee. In the end, New York City suffered $19 billion worth of damage, with New York State needing $41.9 billion worth of repairs, restoration, mitigation, and prevention costs.[132]

Stanton, with his camera, journeyed through the hardest-hit parts of New York City, the surrounding boroughs and the coast, photographing broken landscapes and interviewing as many people as he could. He captured images of bricks torn from walls, plywood strewn into the streets, garbage flung everywhere, wires dangling from dilapidated houses, crooked streetlights and telephone poles ripped off their foundations, and sand mounds on streets. There was destruction everywhere.

Trees and branches had landed on doorsteps of brownstone houses, residential areas, near public housing projects and office buildings alike. Stanton captured the ruins of the houses that burned to the ground in Breezy, Queens. He photographed a group of teenage boys boating around flooded houses, first responders working to save lives, and volunteers who were a part of the debris-clearing operations.[133]

Across the city, he found people working together to clean up the mess. At the center of these efforts was a spirit of camaraderie among people determined to repair their broken neighborhoods.

Confronted with so much wreckage, Stanton, through Humans of New York's Tumblr account, connected with Tumblr founder David Karp. Together they launched a Sandy Relief crowdfunding campaign on Indiegogo.com. The initial goal was to raise $100,000 in ten days.[134] With Stanton's pictures and stories of Humans of New York, the campaign went viral and raised $85,000 in the first twenty-four hours, and $318,530 over the course of ten days.[135]

All the proceeds were donated to the Stephen Siller Tunnel to Towers Foundation, which directly transferred the funds to relief. With the coordination of the Federal Emergency Management Agency (FEMA), they were able to provide funds for sheetrock, flooring, food, cleaning supplies, clothes, and other supplies, which were also given to those in need to help people to get through the fast approaching winter.[136]

This hurricane fundraiser and Stanton's pictures on the Humans of New York page launched him into a role that he could not have imagined when he first moved to New York City jobless and broke. Suddenly, he had a career as a philanthropist. Humans of New York exploded from being a photoblog with a few hundred followers, "to a few thousand, then tens of thousands, and now millions of people" over the course of a few years.

His digital photo and storytelling blog made such an impact that in 2013, *TIME Magazine* named him to its list of "30 People Under 30 Changing the World."[137] He went on to turn Humans of New York into a book, *Humans of New York Stories*, which was published in 2015, followed by a children's book, *Little Humans*. Both became *New York Times* bestsellers.[138]

Stanton began travelling to places around the world on a fifty-day world tour in partnership with the United Nations to tell their stories and to take their pictures. He photographed his way through Pakistan, Iran, Iraq, Congo, Jordan, Uganda, Ukraine, India, Vietnam, and Mexico, to name a few.[139]

Back in New York, he created features with veterans and children battling cancer.

As a student at the University of Georgia, Brandon Stanton would frequently dream of being somebody who could "make a difference." While he could never have imagined how, his dream *did* come true. Humans of New York has drawn together people far beyond New York City to share stories using digital media to portray the common goodness of humanity, as well as its struggles and triumphs.

Today, Humans of New York has well over twenty-five million followers on Instagram and Facebook alone.[140] It has become a digital celebration of the humanity at the heart of America's greatest city.

CHAPTER 22

FIGHTING MALARIA WITH NOTHING BUT NETS

Lynda Commale was at home in Pennsylvania, in the United States, watching a PBS documentary called "Malaria: Fever Wars." The filmmaker, Kevin Hull, had traveled across three continents, including Africa, to capture the devastating spread of malaria through "the perspectives of a few heroic individuals, each fighting their own very different battles against the disease."[141] At that time, a child died from malaria every thirty seconds.

As Commale recalled during an interview, "It was a history and a wonderful educational opportunity to learn about malaria; how it can be prevented and how it can be cured, and it just had triggered such an emotion in me. The information that I had learned truly haunted me, and I knew I had to do something to make this better. My daughter, Katherine, who was five years old, said, 'Mom, let's do something about this. Let's send them some bed nets.'"[142]

"Malaria is a serious and sometimes fatal disease caused by a parasite that commonly infects a certain type of mosquito which feeds on humans."[143]

According to the World Health Organization, "If not treated promptly with effective medicines, malaria can kill by infecting and destroying red blood cells and by clogging the capillaries that carry blood to the brain or other vital organs."[144]

Typically, mosquitoes come out at night. From dusk to dawn, especially when the weather is humid and hot, is the most likely time to contract malaria. Because the mosquitoes' life spans are directly linked to the weather, they thrive and multiply during the rainy seasons when they can lay their eggs in any shallow pools of water, including marshes, swamps, drainage ditches, mud puddles, or even in a footprints or hoof prints left behind after a rain.

The malaria-carrying mosquitoes thrive in hard-to-reach places and poverty-stricken areas where there are no roads, electricity, or other rudimentary infrastructure, let alone window screens. While malaria can be a deadly disease, it also can be prevented. And because it takes but one infected person to start an outbreak, an accurate and swift diagnosis is essential to eradicate malaria and stop it from spreading.

Well over a century ago, almost everywhere in the world, people were at risk of becoming infected by malaria. Today, the number has dropped by nearly 50 percent. While most cases of death occur south of the Sahara Desert in Africa, cases of malaria are still being reported in Latin American, Southeast Asia, and in the Middle East.

Back in Pennsylvania at the Commale home, after speaking with her mother about malaria, five-year-old Katherine Commale wanted to help the people in Africa by sending bed nets to them. "If they have a bed net the mosquitoes can't get them," young Katherine told her mother. "But if they don't, they can get a very bad disease."

While bed nets vary in shapes and sizes, they are nets which hang over people's beds or sleeping mats. "Long-lasting, insecticidal bed nets (LLINs) are a simple, cost-effective solution to protect families from malaria while they sleep. They create a physical barrier against malaria-carrying mosquitoes, and the insecticide woven into the nets kills the mosquitoes before they can transmit the disease from one person to the next."[145]

Katherine and her mother, Lynda, decided to take action to raise awareness about malaria and to raise funds so they could send some lifesaving bed nets to people in Africa and to other countries inflicted with malaria.

Together, they crafted a diorama that had all the touches of a child's imagination. It was a model of a hut made out of pizza boxes. Katherine's three-year-old brother, Joseph, was quick to lend a hand. The children made a little bed to put inside, and then (incongruously) used Katherine's Barbie dolls for the African family who lived in the hut. Toy bugs became the little mosquitoes which they could fly into the hut when the family was sleeping. Tulle ribbon was the bed net.

The Commale family took their diorama to their local church. During their Sunday school classes, they created a simple skit. The children could take turns playing the family or the pesky mosquitoes, or they could be the person who comes out with the bed net and tucks it in around the sleeping family to keep them safe from the mosquitoes.

Katherine asked people to donate ten dollars to buy a bed net to save a life. They raised a rather amazing $2,000. Encouraged, the Commale family kept going to more churches with their skit to bring awareness to the issue of malaria. They donated the funds they received to Nothing-ButNets.net.

Nothing But Nets is an online global grassroots campaign of the United Nations Foundation, established "to raise awareness, funds, and voices to fight malaria." Among their partners is the Bill and Melinda Gates Foundation. The ten dollars donation Katherine sought covers the cost of the insecticide-treated bed net, the delivery of the bed nets to the infected regions, and education for its proper use to prevent malaria.

It was a simple and inexpensive concept to help others in a lifesaving way that resonated with people.

As Lynda Commale explained, "We were able to show them with a tactile experience how a bed net really works—and how a bed net can save a person's life. The kids took to it. The five-year-olds, the six-year-olds, they understood it…and it just grew and grew and grew."[146]

What began as a creative act of charity and compassion in a Pennsylvania home—complete with Barbie-doll African villagers—became a potent force for good thanks to the tools of the Digital Age. Using Web-based marketing, social media campaigns, and traditional media, Katherine's story went global. Within three years, Lynda and Katherine had wildly exceeded their initial goals when they raised over $100,000 for bed nets, while inspiring other students, churches, and athletes to get involved in the fight to eradicate malaria and save lives. As *The New York Times* reported in "A $10 Mosquito Net Is Making Charity Cool":

> *Donating $10 to buy a mosquito net to save an African child from malaria has become a hip way to show you care, especially for teenagers. The movement is like a modern version of the March of Dimes, created in 1938 to defeat polio, or like collecting pennies for UNICEF on Halloween.*

> *Unusual allies, like the Methodist and Lutheran Churches, the National Basketball Association and the United Nations Foundation, are stoking the passion for nets that prevent malaria. The annual "American Idol Gives Back" fund-raising television special has donated about $6 million a year for two years. The music channel VH1 made a fund-raising video featuring a pesky man in a mosquito suit.[147]*

"It just overwhelms my heart," Lynda said when describing the journey that she and her daughter took together when they set out on a journey of compassion. She explains that she asked her then eight-year-old daughter, "Whose goal was it to send 10,000 nets?" Katherine answered, "My mom's!" Lynda then asked, "What is your goal, Katherine?" Her simple but bold reply was, "That everyone in Africa who needs a bed net gets a bed net!"[148]

The Gates Foundation has spent almost $1.2 billion on malaria, and although most goes toward research into vaccines and new drugs, part went to match the first $3 million raised by Nothing But Nets.[149]

In the 2011 Annual Letter from the Gates Foundation, Bill Gates praised Nothing But Nets as well as the type of grassroots campaign that

Katherine and her mom organized to do their part in the fight to prevent malaria, when he wrote:

> In Senegal, where 80 percent of households own a bed net, the number of malaria cases went down 41 percent in a single year. Many amazing grassroots groups are helping with the delivery of bed nets. The Nothing But Nets campaign, for example, has gotten hundreds of thousands of individual citizens and organizations involved in the fight against malaria.[150]

Today, a child dies from malaria every two minutes—a tragic fact but a sign of meaningful progress.

While the fight to eradicate malaria continues, the story of Katherine and her mother affirms the power of individuals to join with others and make a difference—even on the other side of the world—using the tools and resources of the Digital Age.

Getting involved with an organization like the Nothing But Nets program to help defeat malaria or some other scourge on the human condition does not require even as much as the Commale family did. Simply spreading the word via our social media networks can launch digital campaigns and even small contributions can save a life. If a five-year-old like Katherine Commale can engage, so can we.

CHAPTER 23

DIGITAL CRACKS IN CHINA'S GREAT FIREWALL

For centuries, the impressive Great Wall of China served to defend the country from external enemies. With its construction beginning in the third century BC, it embodied the grand vision of the Qin Dynasty's (221 BC–206 BC) first emperor, Qin Shi Huang, to fend off nomadic invaders from the north. Despite the forced labor and the high human toll, it was still an ambitious undertaking that is widely considered as one of the New Seven Wonders of the World.

The parts of the Great Wall that most visitors climb today, which are on the northern outskirts of Beijing, were built during the Ming Dynasty (1368–1644). The Ming boasted vast wealth and numerous technological advantages over medieval Europe, but the rulers continued to build the Great Wall at a time when explosives already had the potential to blast through any such physical barriers. The Ming rulers not only further sealed off China's northern borders but also forbade ships to set sail along China's winding coastline, a policy that continued into the Qing Dynasty (1644–1911). Those policies of seclusion are considered the beginning of China's centuries of relative decline in comparison to European powers committed to a national strategy of exploration and colonization.

Fast forward to the twenty-first century. With the rise of the internet as an indispensable component of human life, the Chinese Communist

Party (CCP) is following the footsteps of China's imperial rulers in erecting a digital Great Wall that censors foreign websites and domestic online content. Commonly known as the "Great Firewall of China," this massive censorship project might be viewed as a strange fusion of the ambition of the Qin Dynasty and the reactionary impulses of the Ming rulers.

The project to censor the internet in China began in the late 1990s and accelerated after the 2008 Beijing Olympics. The majority of the world's most popular websites, such as Google, YouTube, Facebook, Reddit, and Wikipedia, are victims of the Great Firewall—are, as of the writing of this chapter, inaccessible in mainland China. Most foreign social media services are blocked within China because they do not comply with Chinese censorship rules. The same is true of many foreign news websites because they often challenge the CCP's versions of events.[151]

In recent years, internet censorship has become a vast operation that rivals the national defense apparatus of many countries, both in terms of personnel and resources. In 2013, *Beijing News* reported that an officially estimated army of more than *two million* internet police are employed full-time to block unwanted content on websites and monitor communications deemed threatening or critical of the regime.[152] In reality, the actual number today could well be even higher.

In addition to censoring officially-disapproved information and opinions, this vast army of censors is also engaged in promoting propaganda that is designed to confuse or even divert the public from discovering or believing facts that the regime deems threatening.[153] Individuals and organizations that are perceived as challenging the regime's narrative are discredited or demonized in order to taint them.[154] In this way, the world's largest censorship army seeks to target both the message and messenger for any inconvenient truths that leak through the cracks in the firewall.

Finally, in order to ensure unfair odds in the online battle against Chinese citizens, the official censorship army of China is augmented by a huge force of private censorship police employed by major internet companies. Under the Chinese internet censorship system, such companies must sign a pledge to enforce government censorship standards or face being shut down for noncompliance. As a result, every large internet company in China employs a significant number of employees whose role is to implement government censorship policy.[155]

Indeed, the Chinese government has grown so fond of treating the private sector as an extension of their propaganda machine that they even aspire—and often succeed—in forcing foreign companies to self-censor in order to comply with their oppressive demands. Although Taiwan is a democratic society—with a population fiercely committed to their independence—China's demands regarding references to Taiwan are routinely honored by major hotel chains and airlines out of fear of being shut out of the Chinese market.[156] At one level, it seems bizarre that the CCP should work so hard to force the private sector in the West to serve as a de facto propaganda machine for its nationalistic and military claims against a free nation. After all, the tiny nation of Taiwan poses no military or economic threat to mainland China. But such grandiose bullying by the Chinese regime becomes immediately understandable when one considers that a key element of the CCP's claim to legitimacy is the often-repeated falsehood that democracy and human rights are foreign concepts that are antithetical to the Chinese civilization. Taiwan's very existence as a democracy with a vibrant Chinese culture is an obvious rebuke to this falsehood. So, the very name of Taiwan is a threat to the deeply insecure autocrats who have constructed the mythology by which the CCP exercises an oppressive monopoly of power over the people of mainland China.

As the most ambitious censorship project in human history, the Great Firewall of China is also a monument to the CCP's deep need to achieve enforced legitimacy in China through the repression of public opinion. Of course, Chinese authorities can and do play the cultural nationalism card in censoring foreign news media and other non-Chinese sources out of alleged desire to preserve the purity of Chinese society. But most of their effort has actually focused on curbing public discussions on China's domestic social media platforms, where dissenting voices abound. The

CCP obviously feels threatened by the voice that digital media gives to ordinary Chinese citizens—so much so that the regime devotes an astonishing amount of human, technological, and financial capital to the suppression of their views.

On the surface, what the Great Firewall does is censor massive volumes of internet content. The CCP's underlying motive for such a move is to uphold the status quo and to maintain their monopoly on power. Even today, China still shares many of the characteristics of countries in the former Soviet bloc, where totalitarian regimes displayed a phobia for truth and information that they did not control. In the words of the famous Czech leader Václav Havel, China is still "living within a lie."

In the pre-digital era, the façade of the lie in which Chinese people lived was much easier for Chinese Communist authorities to maintain. During most of the Mao era, the Communist Party leadership eliminated Western influences by simply closing off the country to the West. They also harshly persecuted Chinese citizens with alleged Western sympathies through brutal political suppression campaigns. The official CCP narrative, which emphasized communist theories and loyalty to Mao, was then pushed forcibly into every sector of Chinese society and culture. Coupled with the hard power of the state, such intensive campaign of domestic propaganda eliminated nearly all real or perceived challenge to the rule of Mao or the CCP.

After Mao died, the Chinese leadership was able to disentangle from the economic fantasies of 1970s communist theory, initiating capitalist economic reforms that positioned China for economic growth. While economic reforms got under way, comparable political reforms—although supported by a more liberal faction of the CCP in the 1980s—never occurred. Any hope for political progress to mirror China's economic reforms came to an abrupt halt in 1989 when Deng Xiaoping crushed pro-democracy student protesters in Tiananmen Square.

The ensuing official lie the state began to promote is the myth of "socialism with Chinese characteristics." But behind this rhetorical veil of nationalism and patriotism is an oppressive reality that requires the world's greatest censorship apparatus to suppress. Below the level of public rhetoric, the reality is that the system has become a state of oligarchy that involves rampant corruption and crony capitalism, as well as heightening authoritarian controls of all aspects of society.

The rise of the internet threatened the CCP's monopoly of information as well as its official narrative of untruths. As Havel points out in his famous essay "The Power of the Powerless," any single challenge to the post-totalitarian lie is a threat to the *entire* system. Social systems founded upon lies require massive exertion to maintain. The system must crush even small expressions of truth—such as the views of ordinary citizens—since self-preservation requires such an automatic response of repression.

Indeed, as the most extensive and sophisticated program of national censorship in human history, the Great Firewall is a tribute to the magnitude of the lie within which the Chinese people are forced to live, forgoing the basic human aspiration of seeking truth. In this way, the Great Firewall is a monument to the reality that the Chinese regime fears its own people—and the truth—more than its external enemies.

Since assuming power in late 2012, President Xi Jinping has exercised an ever-tightening politics of control, squeezing out civil society, cracking down on dissent, strengthening the rule of the CCP, and leading China on a path of centralized, authoritarian rule unseen since Mao. After amassing power in his first five-year term, President Xi recently revoked the term limit on his tenure under the Chinese constitution—a legal protection previously put in place to prevent the rise of another dictator like Mao.

The full carnage and destruction that flowed from Mao's dictatorship—culminating in the notorious Cultural Revolution—is still not discussed or studied openly in China. Nonetheless, there is enough collective memory of the suffering of this era—which touched the lives of every Chinese family—that the dangerous implications of these developments have not been lost on many Chinese. But when Chinese netizens attempted to point out the downsides of Xi's ruler-for-life ambitions, the full force of the Great Firewall was unleashed against all criticism and even parody of President Xi's pretensions. Such was the intense nervousness of the Chinese authorities that even the most innocent parodies of Xi were censored. For example, all images of Winnie-the-Pooh were quashed wherever it was suspected that Chinese netizens were using the chubby cartoon figure to refer to Xi.[157] Such is the reach of the long arm of Xi's censorship army that foreign media have also been penalized for even mentioning this revealing display of paranoia and insecurity by the CCP. HBO has been blocked in China because of John Oliver's audacity in making humorous reference to the story.[158] Now the latest Disney Winnie-the-Pooh movie has also been banned from the Chinese market for fear that showing the film might reignite public discussion of Xi's pretensions to lifetime dictatorship in the infamous pattern of Mao.[159]

The history of all societies—particularly ancient and complex societies—cannot be foretold by mere mortals. So, we would do well to acknowledge that the future of China is still an open book. But in the long run, the world's greatest censorship machine can only succeed if it totally eliminates ideas and opinions that challenge the falsehoods of the Communist Party's narrative. A few cracks in the Great Firewall are all that is needed to let in the truth. We have a reasonable hope that the trends that we are describing will continue.

Specifically, we must hope that in spite of the fact the Chinese regime has increased its internet censorship under President Xi, China's censors are fighting a losing battle. In recent years, despite redoubled effort to censor information on the internet, Chinese netizens have shown signs of resolve on China's social media platforms and successfully raised awareness on numerous social issues. As more and more people get to access information and ideas challenging those of the government's, the cracks in China's Great Firewall are growing.

The issues that garner the widest attention—and sometimes trigger the most outrage—relate to product safety, especially food and medicine. Before social media became popular in China, the authorities had an easier time censoring information, and thus controlling public discussion, by relying mostly on censorship of the traditional press. Nearly all the media organizations in China are state-owned, and even those that are independent in name are under tight state control. The Central Propaganda Department oversees all press contents and dictates the good news to report on and the negative information to avoid. Journalists who test the limits of censorship are often silenced.

In 2010, Chinese journalist Wang Keqin reported that at least four children had died and dozens more were sickened after being injected with vaccines that were left unrefrigerated by government officials to keep the labels from peeling. Amid official denials, the government ordered other media to downplay the story. Wang was subsequently forced to resign from two Chinese newspapers and faced death threats, but he continued to blog. His publisher, Bao Yueyang, was fired for defending him.

In such cases, whether or not to allow the story to develop is often a political decision. For example, in 2007, Zheng Xiaoyu, who was head of China's State Food and Drug Administration from 2003 to 2005, received the death penalty for corruption and allowing possibly tainted products to be sold in China. Such a harsh and highly publicized move was carefully staged to protect the reputation of the regime and send a propaganda message. However, the following year the Sanlu milk powder scandal broke right after the Beijing Olympics, indicating that not much had actually changed.

Even when such cases are publicized in the traditional media, the public coverage follows a propaganda script that deflects blame from the government and positions Chinese authorities as the heroes. Excuses such as "China is still a developing country" and "the government is doing its best" fill the public media rhetoric. For this reason, one can find Chinese people who still echo such sentiments today—even after the passage of time has rendered such arguments increasingly dubious. Of course, the reality is that such scripted excuses cannot remedy the fundamental flaws of China's regulatory structure—a monopolistic top-down power structure that lacks public oversight and accountability. For this reason, the structures for regulating product safety in China remain permanently vulnerable to repeated offenses and scandals.

Some argue that social media has not fared much better than traditional media in spreading information and ideas that challenge official propaganda in China. However, the sheer volume of social media communications in the world's largest market mean that the social media censors are constantly playing catch-up with the speed of information flow on the internet. On the one hand, in addition to the world's largest censorship army, the Great Firewall now employs advanced technologies that can filter and block sensitive keywords from spreading. But whereas a banned article would never appear in traditional media, mass censorship of social media usually does not occur before millions of users have already seen the censored materials. Therefore, as social media becomes more ubiquitous in Chinese society, it is reasonable to assume that more people will continue to share information and opinions on scandals—often in spite of the online censorship regime. Amazingly, in spite of facing the biggest government censorship Goliath in the world, some Digital Davids in China have been able to achieve what the brave journalist Wang Keqin could not—to raise awareness for China's pharmaceutical scandals on a mass scale.

In 2016, more than three dozen people were arrested in a trafficking ring involving $90 million worth of expired vaccines for polio, chickenpox, rabies, and other diseases that had been stored at improper temperatures. The expired vaccines had been sold in twenty-four Chinese provinces. Public outrage erupted on WeChat and Weibo, the most popular Chinese social media services similar to WhatsApp and Twitter. Government censors directed state media to downplay the story after Chinese premier Li Keqiang promised to crack down on violators.

Before social media, scandals that broke on traditional media were carefully controlled "explosions" that did not hurt the image of the Chinese regime, in spite of the fact that Chinese authorities were almost always ultimately responsible. Indeed, such traditional media might even be cynically enlisted by authorities to stage a carefully scripted "resolution" to the scandal involving concerned government officials suddenly "discovering" the problem and then heroically resolving it. This all changed with the advent of social media where—even in China—people have begun to partially break the monopoly of the traditional press on the flow of information. Social media not only allowed people to share the news of the scandals but also enabled them to share their opinion and frustration. Instead of buying the promises by politicians, more and more people are listening to each other and choosing to believe what they learn from other citizens, even if it deviates from the official narrative. Although many people still have faith in the Chinese government, scandal after scandal on social media are gradually exposing more and more people to the lies of the system.

Unsurprisingly, Li's promise eventually rang hollow, because the problematic regulatory structure was never substantially reformed. In July 2018, another pharmaceutical scandal broke out, but this time it was first revealed on social media.

On the social network WeChat, a blogger using the penname "King of the Beasts" reported that Changsheng Bio-Technology Co. had distributed more than 252,000 ineffective doses of vaccine for diphtheria, whooping cough, and tetanus. According to the *South China Morning Post*, the Chinese government confirmed that more than 215,000 of those DPT doses were administered to children. Changsheng was also found to have falsified records for more than 113,000 doses of rabies vaccine. The blogger is not an independent investigator; the information was available on a government agency website, but no one took the initiative to publicize the information in the media before the blogger did.

The blogger's report—alleging decades of corruption—went viral as Chinese parents feared for the safety of their children, who must receive the free inoculations to attend school. Reuters reported that a hashtag on the vaccine scandal was read more than 600 million times in a matter of days.

Outrage that parents initially directed at the company was soon also being directed at government officials, who were deemed untrustworthy at best and unaccountably corrupt at worst. Many used Weibo and WeChat to declare that they no longer trusted Chinese products and would only purchase foreign-made vaccines. Travel bookings to Hong Kong, where clinics use only foreign vaccines, soared, with tens of thousands seeking appointments. Some clinics said they were booked solid for months.

Chinese censors took down the blogger's viral post within a day, but the word was out and the government felt compelled to take action to quell the swelling anger. Police moved to arrest the chairperson of Changsheng and seventeen other people involved in the case. The company was also fined over 3.4 million yuan ($500,000) for distributing the DPT vaccines.

Another pharmaceutical company, the government-owned Wuhan Institute of Biological Products, was fined after being accused of producing 400,000 substandard vaccine doses. The lack of arrests in that case prompted suspicion that it received lesser punishment as a government enterprise.

Such is the rage of the Chinese people at these developments that even the man who aspires to a lifetime of dictatorship, thanks to the monopolistic and authoritarian system that produced the scandal, is now striving to save face by rhetorically distancing himself from it. President Xi Jinping, who was on a tour of Africa, called the scandal "vile and shocking." He said corruption should be met with harsh punishment "to cure the chronic disease and scratch poison from one's bones." He ordered officials to "improve the supervision of vaccines and guard the bottom line of safety in order to safeguard public interest and social security."

Premier Li Keqiang, just as he did after the vaccine scandal in 2016, again pledged that the government would "resolutely crack down on all illegal and criminal acts that endanger the safety of people's lives." Li also charged a Chinese manufacturer of faulty vaccines with crossing "a moral bottom line." While such resolute statements by Xi and his subordinates may inspire some of the public, many Chinese are well aware that past efforts to purge corruption were largely used to purge Xi's rivals from positions of power. Indeed, that now points the finger of blame all the more clearly in the direction of the CCP and the current leadership of the government.

But what is moral or immoral in an officially atheistic country? Since the 1980s, China has enjoyed spectacular material success by allowing a degree of economic freedom—while refusing to allow political freedom and a wide range of basic rights that are fundamental to the legal systems of the developed nations of the world. In many cases this has created a moral vacuum where material success is the single overarching goal. And in the absence of opposition parties or an independent judiciary, Communist Party favorites can escape regulation and accountability. This is the dilemma faced by an awakening citizenry that was taught to trust its leaders. But the people's concerns can no longer be ignored, even inside China's Great Firewall.

Bob Fu, founder and chairman of US-based China Aid, which advocates for religious freedom and the rule of law in China, says faulty vaccines peddled for profit are "the poisoned fruit" of atheistic one-party control. But he says not even China's internet surveillance and control can squelch parents' outrage over hundreds of thousands of flawed vaccine doses administered to their children.

State media appealed for calm, offering unproven assurances that any of the faulty vaccines administered to children as young as three months old would be merely ineffective and not harmful. But many parents were unconvinced.

A woman whose one-year-old daughter had received a vaccine made by Changsheng told *The New York Times*, "We always say that kids are the nation's future." But now, she said, "We don't know who we can believe in." She vowed to purchase any future vaccines from abroad because, "Getting hurt again and again has made us lose faith."

CNN reported that a parent outside the Capital Institute of Pediatrics in Beijing said the company had "no conscience" and that stricter government regulation was needed.

The following week, more than two dozen parents boldly protested outside the headquarters of the National Health Commission in Beijing, holding banners and chanting "Justice for the victims!" To an observer in the West, a protest by several dozen people may not seem particularly impressive. But in mainland China public protests are exceedingly rare—with police responding aggressively to even a single public protestor. As a result, a protest of this size is extraordinary and speaks volumes about public sentiment.

An initial torrent of online protests against the vaccine manufacturers was permitted, but firewall enforcers soon moved to bring the swelling controversy under control. They made the word "vaccine" one of the most restricted words on Weibo and took down critical articles and comments. Many messages and articles were saved, however, by viewers who attached them to digital blockchains that were unreachable by censors.

Futurism Magazine reports that internet users sent themselves about forty-seven cents worth of the digital asset Ether and posted critical articles in the metadata of the transaction. Futurism notes that, "Because the Ethereum blockchain is a public ledger, anyone can view this transaction (and read the included article)." It adds that, "The ledger is also decentralized, so there's no single authority Chinese officials could pressure to remove the article."

One of the most viewed commentaries on the vaccine scandal was posted by human rights lawyer Zhang Kai, whose arrest three years earlier had caused an international outcry. Zhang was detained after defending churches that were being forced to remove their crosses and crucifixes. Officials in Zhejiang Province—a province with a large Christian population—had called for the removal or demolition of more than 1,200 crosses in hundreds of parishes.

Zhang was taken into custody on August 25, 2015, the day before he was scheduled to meet with Rabbi David Saperstein, who was, at that time, the US Ambassador at Large for International Religious Freedom. Chinese officials accused Zhang, a Christian, of organizing illegal religious gatherings, "gathering a crowd to disturb public order" and "endangering state secrets." He was held for almost seven months and was only released after making a televised confession, which supporters believe he made under duress.

Now living in Beijing where he blogs for a living but is barred from practicing law, Zhang recalled his efforts to publicize the initial vaccine scandal back in 2010, saying interviews that he posted online were quickly censored. He wrote that in the following year he met with many families whose children had received faulty vaccines. "After finishing the treatment," he wrote, "many of the children would suffer sudden seizures and some even died," although officials attributed their deaths to other causes.

Zhang says some victims of the tainted vaccines went to court in 2010, but their cases were thrown out. They then took their complaints to the Department of Health, only to be detained there for protesting. Zhang says he then "took up their cause and brought an administrative lawsuit." Facing rejection in that case, Zhang says he argued with the judge and was thrown out of court. He says some people who complained were sentenced to up to two years in prison on grounds that they were just trying to cause trouble.

Zhang compared China's handling of vaccine scandals to similar cases in the United States, noting differences in corporate accountability and legal standards of evidence, burden of proof, and compensation. He concluded that in China, "our children are more than ten times more likely to be disabled or killed by vaccines when compared to American children, while the compensation is more than ten times less than in the United States."

A photojournalist identified as Guo Xianzhong also spent several years traveling around China interviewing fifty families whose children received the faulty vaccines. His report features heartbreaking video of severely disabled children and interviews with their parents, who say they received little or no compensation and cannot sue the government. Some of the parents said their children had died.

Reflecting on China's more recent vaccine problems and the lack of accountability, Zhang Kai wrote that he felt like a helpless passenger on a huge rocking ship and that all of the Chinese people are in the same listing boat, being tossed about wherever it goes.

He adds that most of the lawyers who helped vaccine victims in years past are no longer practicing and wonders, "Where are they now?" Many, like him, were arrested and stripped of their law licenses in a 2015 crackdown. Those who are left, Zhang says, can often do little more than comfort the victims.

In comparison, the social media awareness campaign against faulty vaccines resulted in more success than efforts by journalists, lawyers, and activists amid China's rampant censorship and harsh crackdowns on activism in the civil society.

There are not many digital cracks in the Great Firewall—since the Communist Party expends vast resources to close them—but those that exist offer a window into a reality that is very different from the official propaganda narrative, which falsely covers up deep social problems and proclaims that all is well.

The story of *Human Liberty 2.0* is happening on a global scale, but some countries such as China pose particularly serious challenges. Indeed, it would be foolish to underestimate the tenacity and longevity of the Chinese regime. Unlike other cases around the world in which people sometimes achieve tangible near-term success with the use of technology, China's citizen-driven social media revolution against the world's greatest censorship regime will be a long uphill battle.

In the meantime, the Chinese regime's campaign to promote public ignorance and indoctrination through the Great Firewall may ultimately prove to be a losing battle. The speed and the rate at which social media exposes Chinese people to uncensored information, despite the fact that much of such information gets censored in the end, are gradually pulling the citizenry out of the orbit of official propaganda. While this process is slow, every day more and more people are coming to the realization that the true culprit for all the scandals is the system itself, which the Chinese authorities are desperately trying to uphold for their own benefit at the expense of the Chinese people. Once individuals achieve that realization, they will never look back.

Zhang noted that a former classmate of his who became a successful businessman said his goal now was to make enough money so that his son can leave China and live abroad. Apparently, many other Chinese feel the same way, since online searches for information about emigration from China have spiked dramatically in the wake of the latest vaccine scandals—in the same way they did after President Xi abolished all constitutional limits on his power. But, of course, news coverage of such facts has also been suppressed by the Chinese censors, along with search terms such as "migration" and "emigration, for at least a period of time."[160]

Needless to say, such developments are the final ironic comment on the degree to which the Great Firewall reverses the original purpose for the Great Wall of China. Whereas the Great Wall was intended to defend China from foreign invaders, the Great Firewall exists to defend the power and privilege of the Communist Party from the Chinese people. To the extent that this truth leaks through the firewall, it has the potential to make the existing cracks larger and harder to close.

Oppressive regimes create walls against freedom and want everyone—on both sides—to accept them as eternal. Indeed, there are many in the West who rush to defend the proposition that the Great Firewall—along with other aspects of the repressive legal and political system in China—must be accepted as an embodiment of Chinese cultural norms. After all, authoritarianism has been a feature of Chinese society for generations. These same voices deride the notion that "western" legal concepts such as freedom of speech will ever become a reality in China.

But those of us on the outside of the Great Firewall cannot forget the humanity of our brothers and sisters on the inside. In reality, we fail in our fundamental duty as members of the human family when we allow such deeply deluded excuses for oppression to deny the fundamental dignity and rights of the Chinese people. It is a self-evident truth that the principles of universal rights are for everyone, everywhere, at all times—or they mean nothing at all.

Many people, both inside and outside of the Soviet Union, believed that the Berlin Wall—and all the oppression that it symbolized—would never fall. Indeed, there were many who argued that the free world should not press the Soviet Union on human rights issues precisely for this reason. But in reality, such walls tend to collapse when they can no longer contain the force of the truths that undermine their public legitimacy. Let us hope that this process is now underway in China. Even if we may not see it in our lifetime, those of us who believe in *Human Liberty 2.0* must work for the day when future generations of Chinese can celebrate their freedom in the rubble of the Great Firewall.

CHAPTER 24

PRIVACY RIGHTS VIOLATIONS IN THE PRE-DIGITAL AGE

If the internet had a conscience, it would be Joe Cannataci.

He is a multilingual professor, an extraordinary global diplomat, an expert on the intersection of law and technology, and an unremitting defender for one of the most poorly understood, yet critically vital human rights—the fundamental right to privacy. But while he has been a passionate and relentless promoter of human rights and especially privacy, he is most self-effacing when it comes to his own role in that struggle. As a result, few know about his leadership role in crafting a steady stream of legislation that has given his home region of Europe far more online privacy protection than the United States—a reality that is both ironic and frightening, given the historical dominance of US companies in shaping the landscape of the internet.

While Professor Cannataci is a proud citizen of his home country of Malta, and a longstanding member of the University of Malta's faculty—the place he began his career fighting to advance the cause of privacy rights in the realm of technology—he also now serves as the UN Special Rapporteur on the right to privacy. While perhaps a more prestigious position from which to engage in the daunting global battle to keep the internet from becoming everyone's worst nightmare, the fact is that Connataci has dedicated much of his professional life to helping governments understand and close the gap between pre-digital legal systems designed to protect fundamental, universal human rights, such as privacy, and the technological realities that are inevitably advancing at an exponential pace and, in the process, infringing on those rights.

"If privacy," says Professor Cannataci, "like freedom from torture or so many other rights, is a fundamental human right, then it is also a universal right, which means that everybody all over the world has the right to privacy, irrespective of where he or she may be, irrespective of whatever passport he or she may hold."[161]

We'll look at that gap Connataci has been working on a bit more in the next chapter, but for now, it is important to bear in mind this important point: all technology is morally neutral. It can be used for good or for evil. Pharmaceutical drugs can be used to save your life or can turn you into a drug addict. Nuclear power can give light to a city or destroy it. The same is true of the internet. As we have seen in the pages of this book, the internet can be used to connect, to inform, to teach, and to liberate—or it can be used to spread propaganda, recruit terrorists, or oppress an entire population by invading their privacy. The crucial question is how to foster the former while preventing the latter. Finding the answer is no easy task.

When it comes to digital culture, one of the most dangerous trends of our age is the growing invasion of individual privacy by powerful actors—including governments and corporations—who can harness the power of digital surveillance technology and big data to monitor, control, manipulate, and even target and persecute ordinary people. As digital technology expands its reach into even the smallest crevices of our lives and world, the accelerating loss of privacy poses a real threat to the efforts of human beings to use the internet for good. Indeed, without the right to privacy, a whole host of closely-related fundamental rights can be lost. That is why the efforts of Cannataci and other privacy rights champions are so critical for the overall progress of what we are calling *Human Liberty 2.0*.

For *Human Liberty 2.0* to advance to the fullest, though, the world must have voices that push back against the dark forces that seek to use the internet in ways that violate human dignity, including your privacy. This is imperative so the human rights champions who we have been profiling in *Human Liberty 2.0*—and future generations of Digital Davids who will follow them—can continue their work on behalf of all of humanity.

Cannataci is one of those voices leading the charge. But in an age of fashionable self-promotion, Cannataci has done little to draw attention to himself or to seek accolades.

The United Nations creates "Special Rapporteurs" to champion particularly important human rights issues on a global scale. When the UN decided to create the office of Special Rapporteur on the right to privacy, Cannataci was a logical choice.[162] In addition to other academic appointments, Cannataci is the head of his university's Department of Information Policy & Governance of the Faculty of Media and Knowledge Sciences. He was also a driving force behind the protection of digital privacy in Europe.[163]

Even before the World Wide Web was invented, Professor Cannataci had been warning about the dangers of what can happen when people are deprived of their privacy rights. In 1986, he made this farsighted statement regarding privacy and autonomy:

> *Shorn of the cloak of privacy that protects him, an individual becomes transparent and therefore manipulable. A manipulable individual is at the mercy of those who control the information held about him, and his freedom, which is often relative at best, shrinks in direct proportion to the extent of the nature of the options and alternatives which are left open to him by those who control the information.*
>
> *Autonomy, or the right to or condition of self-governance, is defined as "the freedom from external control or influence; independence."[164]*

In an interview for this book, Professor Cannataci made it clear he "does not like to be manipulated by anyone." Moreover, he does not like to see others in any country, under any circumstances being manipula -ted, either.

It is axiomatic that those who care most passionately about human rights are most often those who have had their rights denied or who have otherwise witnessed first-hand the suffering that ensues when governments disregard fundamental human rights.

Although he does not speak about it a great deal in public, as a student Cannataci was a democracy advocate in his home country of Malta during a period of extremely hardline socialist control of the small island nation. In fact, at one point he felt it necessary to move away from his island home due to the attention he had garnered as a visible campus leader advocating for political reform. Fortunately, he was eventually able to return when the socialist regime that he had fought against disappeared into the dustbin of history.

George Orwell's *1984*

Professor Cannataci is arguably the most dangerous kind of prophet—a charming, urbane intellectual with the heart of a human rights champion. Beneath his polished exterior is a radical with a dangerous instinct for challenging the dehumanizing systems of power and authority that intimidates almost everyone else.

In today's digital era, Cannataci is probably best described as the closest thing to a reincarnated George Orwell, in light of the fact that both gave visionary warnings about the dangers of privacy rights and human rights abuses, which go hand in glove.

In the pre-digital era, British writer and journalist George Orwell prophetically warned in his masterpiece, the dystopian novel, *1984*, that in the future the dignity of individual human beings would be increasingly at risk of being crushed by the power of large organizations, and particularly the state.

1984, told through the eyes of the fictional protagonist, Winston Smith, a simple, everyday person who dared to question the State's growing and intrusive power, was published on June 8, 1949, in the UK, shortly before Orwell's tragic early death of tuberculosis at the age of forty-six, in January 1950.

Orwell, like Professor Cannataci, loathed any system that constrains free thought and intimidates and manipulates people into self-censorship. He warned against the dreadful consequences that would follow when people are forced to live under totalitarian authority with omnipresent surveillance. As Orwell famously and ominously wrote in *1984*: "Big Brother is watching you."

Orwell was born on June 25, 1903. He grew up at a time when television and airplanes were invented. He had lived through World War I and World War II. He saw the rise of the Nazi dictator, "*Mein* Führer," Chancellor Adolf Hitler, and his Third Reich in Germany; fascism in Italy under "*Il Duce*," Benito Mussolini; Chairman Mao Zedong's communist revolution in China; and communism under Supreme Leader Joseph Stalin's Soviet Union. All these so-called "leaders for the people," as they had repeatedly claimed to be, in grim reality ended up becoming murderous dictators. During what became reigns of terror, these dictators, by abusing the resources of the State, sought total and absolute control over everything and everyone. Human rights and privacy rights were ruthlessly ignored to keep them in power. As an astute observer, Orwell was keenly aware of the social injustice that resulted from the violation of the privacy rights of others, and he foresaw that one of the central mechanisms for oppression would be the total invasion of the private lives of citizens by the State. As he chillingly described Big Brother in *1984*: "Always eyes watching you and the voice enveloping you. Asleep or awake, indoors or out of doors, in the bath or bed—no escape. Nothing was your own except the few cubic centimeters in your skull."[165]

This is not the Big Brother of the long running popular TV series, a hybrid reality TV game show where contestants volunteer to live together temporarily in a custom-built fancy house loaded with amenities wired with cameras as they compete for prizes. No, what Orwell was describing is living under a totalitarian Big Brother regime every day for the rest of your life where there are no prizes at the end.

Orwell coined some fictional terms that are still used and familiar today: "Big Brother," "newspeak," "doublethink," and "thought crimes." They are especially relevant now, in the digital age, with regard to privacy rights. Under totalitarian regimes, "Big Brother," the state, was also known as "The Party." The Party dealt with dissent by crushing it, stripping people of their privacy rights, freedom of expression, and all other human rights, until dissidents became "unpersons," a term used to dehumanize those who didn't agree.

He defined "doublethink":

The power of holding two contradictory beliefs in one's mind simultaneously, and accepting both of them. ...To tell deliberate lies while genuinely believing in them, to forget any fact that has become inconvenient, and then, when it becomes necessary again, to draw it back from oblivion for just as long as it is needed, to deny the existence of objective reality and all the while to take account of the reality which one denies—all this is indispensably necessary. Even in using the word doublethink it is necessary to exercise doublethink. For by using the word one admits that one is tampering with reality; by a fresh act of doublethink one erases this knowledge; and so on indefinitely, with the lie always one leap ahead of the truth.[166]

Orwell's fictional language, "newspeak," was intentionally manipulative. It redefined words to lessen the negative impact of their original meaning and intent. For instance "bad" became "ungood," "warm" became "uncold," and as aforementioned, "dissidents" were dehumanized and became "unpersons," and so forth. The Party's drumbeat slogans turned reality on its head, forcing their citizens to believe the unbelievable. The Party's slogans proclaimed:

WAR IS PEACE

FREEDOM IS SLAVERY

IGNORANCE IS STRENGTH

Little by little, bit by bit, doublethink and newspeak made it easier for the officials and officers of The Party, without apparent care or conscience, to violate people's privacy and human rights.

"Thought criminal" was a term Orwell used in his novel when he was describing a person who, according to The Party, was thinking socially unacceptable thoughts, who held opinions that were ideologically different from the official orthodoxy. "The Party takes loyalty seriously," Orwell wrote, "and does not tolerate any acts of subversion—even if they are mere thoughts."[167] And what was the process to discover what the Party considered to be thought crimes? *Invade people's privacy.*

The Harvard philosopher and writer George Santayana wisely and famously said, "Those who cannot remember the past are condemned to repeat it." So, to chart a course to keep the internet as a tool for good, and to understand the importance of the work Professor Cannataci and others like him are doing around the world to protect your privacy rights in the digital era, it is worth learning from history how violations of privacy rights due to constant surveillance were used to violate human rights more broadly in the pre-digital age. Let's briefly revisit, then, the real-life police state of East Germany under the rule of the Socialist Unity Party of Germany and its hated secret police known as the Stasi.

East Germany's Stasi Police-State

Before the digital era of surveillance, hackers, and data collection, East Germany's Ministry for State Security—the "Stasis" (*Staatssicherheitsdienst*) or secret police—was what East Germans feared and detested most. Nicknamed "the Sword and Shield of the Party," the Stasi specialized in surveillance. In the annals of history, the word "Stasi" has become an infamous synonym for police terror. The Stasi's fierce tactics kept East German citizens contained, fearful, obedient, self-censoring, and docile behind the Berlin Wall.

The Berlin Wall was the physical and ideological divide between West Germany, the Federal Republic of Germany (FRG), and East Germany, the German Democratic Republic (GDR), a satellite state of the communist Soviet Union. Under a decree passed by East Germany's unicameral legislature, the Volkskammer, or "the People's Chamber," the Berlin Wall was erected in 1961. It was built to block East Germans, mainly professionals, intellectuals, academics, and skilled workers from fleeing East Germany for the freedoms and opportunities in West Germany under the FRG.

Between 1949 and 1961, approximately 2.5 million East Germans had left for the West. Their departure was threatening East Germany's economic stability and sustainability.

The original [Berlin] wall built of barbed wire and cinder blocks, was subsequently replaced by a series of concrete walls (up to 15 feet [5 meters] high) that were topped with barbed wire and guarded with watchtowers, gun emplacements, and mines. By the 1980s that system of walls, electrified fences, and fortifications extended 28 miles (45 km) through Berlin, dividing the two parts of the city, and extended a further 75 miles (120 km) around West Berlin, separating it from the rest of East Germany.[168]

The Berlin Wall was also known, as Sir Winston Churchill metaphorically called it, as the Iron Curtain. It symbolized the Cold War. It epitomized the communism of the East, with its strict Marxist ideology, and stood in stark contrast to the freedom-loving democracies in the West.

The Stasi was notorious for the intrusive surveillance they conducted of their own citizens in an effort to suffocate and eradicate dissent against GDR's communist regime. While citizens were at work, for example, and there were no sounds coming from the neighbors, Stasi officers and operatives would pick the front door locks, or use skeleton keys to open the deadbolts of targeted apartments and homes to conduct clandestine searches. Once inside, they would lock the door from the inside, and have security officers posted outside to run interference in case the residents who lived there returned home early.

Reminiscent of Orwell's fictional *Thought Police* ("Thinkpol"), while inside, the Stasi would search through the unsuspecting resident's belongings, taking Polaroid photographs and making lists or copies of anything important, useful, or suspicious—various personal or professional documents, passports, poems, calendars, notes, manuscripts—anything they considered to be harmful to society and/or unacceptable to the GDR's communist regime.

These Statsi officers and operatives would depart without leaving a trace, so the individuals who lived there would have no idea their home had been broken into and searched. Thereafter, it was easy for the Statsi to arrest them. Academics, writers, lawyers, journalists, actors, and sports figures were viewed as threats if they could not be co-opted by the State to do its bidding.

In some cases, the Stasi's insidious operatives would break into citizen's homes and run wires through the walls or electrical sockets connected to recording devices at one end and tiny microphones or telephone bugs at the other. This is one method the Stasi used to monitor people's activities. Another was to infiltrate government agencies and civil society institutions: Workplaces, social clubs, universities, schools, government offices—there were spies everywhere. Life in GDR meant your private mail was routinely opened and the government didn't even bother to conceal it. The citizens knew they were being watched. As a result, self-censorship reigned supreme for self-preservation purposes while advancing the state-system.

This outrageous, perpetual privacy rights-violating conduct was in blatant contravention of Article 19 of the Universal Declaration of Human Rights referenced earlier, which states: "Everyone has the right to freedom of opinion and expression; this right includes freedom to hold opinions without interference and to seek, receive and impart information and ideas through any media and regardless of frontiers."

In the communist GDR, jeans were forbidden clothing to wear until the 1970s. Travel outside of the GDR required permission from the State. Individuals who could not obtain permission to travel and tried to escape rarely succeeded in getting past the thousands of armed East German guards patrolling the wall or the checkpoints, the anti-vehicle ditches, or the other booby traps. Those who tried and failed were arrested or shot. One incredibly daring and rare successful escape from the GDR occurred in 1979. It involved a hot air balloon. Hans Strelczyk and Gunter Wetzel, a mechanic and a mason, used their mechanical skills to build a hot air balloon engine out of old propane cylinders. Meanwhile, their industrious wives made a makeshift balloon out of scraps of canvas and old bed sheets like a giant quilt. Together with their four children, the Strelczyk and Wetzel families in their makeshift hot air balloon literally floated up thousands of feet in East Germany and drifted "across the wall of fortifications, minefields, self-firing explosives and guard towers," to precious freedom in the West. They landed near the Bavarian town of Naila, where locals offered them clothes, food, money, apartments, and jobs.

"Once again, human ingenuity and the insatiable desire to be freed had prevailed over communist East Germany's determination to immure its citizens behind arguably the most formidable frontier in history."[169]

There were no privacy rights that the Stasi did not invade. They listened in on personal conversations, monitored sexual habits, looked for anything that could be perceived as disloyal or incriminating. Extramarital affairs were used for easy blackmail and compliance. All the while the Stasi spies diligently kept typed reports and created files on their fellow countrymen. Who visited whom and when. A negative comment or opinion could result in an individual's career trajectory being permanently derailed.

Neighbors were recruited to spy on neighbors. Eavesdropping and informing became part of normal life for millions of the citizenry in East Germany in a society controlled and under constant surveillance by the State. While the numbers vary, reportedly one in ninety East Germans provided information and worked unofficially as *"inoffizielle Mitarbeiter"* (informal collaborators) for the secret police.[170] This made the Stasi's job even easier and helped to establish a permanent spying mechanism of daily reporting for the Stasi police state. Children were not immune from persecution either. While some citizens were die-hard believers in the GDR's communist state, others did the Stasi's bidding because of coercion and manipulation. Still others had their own ulterior reasons—jealousy, revenge, to receive rewards and perks from the State to make their lives a little more comfortable, etc. Indeed, family members, friends, lovers, brothers and sisters, and even husbands and wives turned on one another. Quickly a person could be labeled "GM," for "*gute Menschen*," which means "good people," or "BM," "*brauchbare Menschen*," or "unusable people."

As Christhard Läpple, an author and reporter for German television station ZDF, wrote in his book, *Betrayal Has No Expiration Date*:

> *Most of the spies interviewed professed to be committed socialists who believed they were weeding out capitalist opponents. But others were simply remorseless opportunists with scant regard for the lives they ruined. All withheld their real names for fear of being ostracized.*
>
> *One boy, identified as Dieter, was betrayed by his own teacher for daring to ask in a school lesson: "If East Germany are the goodies, why did we build the Berlin Wall?" Dieter was dispatched to a children's home where food deprivation and beatings were commonplace, before he was eventually "sold" to West Germany for hard currency in 1983. Now living in Hamburg, eking out a living as a tour-bus driver, Dieter expressed no bitterness for his lost youth, however, and no regret for his actions.*
>
> *"Without people like us, the Wall would still be there," he said.[171]*

For his book and documentary programs for ZDF, Läpple spent four years going through Statsi files and interviewing ex-spies and their victims.

When the Berlin Wall fell the night of November 9, 1989, after weeks of civil unrest, it was in large part due to the dissidents fighting for their human and privacy rights and the right to live free from the

Stasi's surveillance and prying eyes. Finally, government officials had no choice but to lift travel restrictions and to open the Wall. Once they did, swarms of people with nothing but the clothes on their backs rushed to get through it. The Berlin Wall came down almost as quickly as it was built.

Without individuals, activists, dissidents like young Dieter, the Strelczyk and Wetzel families, and countless others of all ages and genders standing up against the GDR's Socialist Unity Party of Germany in a pursuit of freedom, millions of people potentially would still be living without with their basic human and privacy rights in East Germany and the Soviet Union.

In clear juxtaposition to the practices of the Stasi, the right to privacy is a basic human right. As the Universal Declaration of Human Rights Article 12 states:

No one shall be subjected to arbitrary interference with his privacy, family, home or correspondence, nor to attacks upon his honour and reputation. Everyone has the right to the protection of the law against such interference or attacks.

Today in the digital era of data mining, digital profiling, metadata, and mass surveillance, where people are nonchalantly surrendering their privacy rights without a second thought—rights that the dissidents of the former GDR and Soviet Union fought so hard to get back—stalwart defenders of those rights, such as Professor Cannataci, are both sounding the alarm and issuing a clarion call to join them in working to protect privacy rights for all on the internet. In the next chapter, you will see how this directly affects you and everyone you love.

CHAPTER 25

PRIVACY RIGHTS IN THE DIGITAL SURVEILLANCE ERA

I t's a truism that if something on the internet is *free* the product is *you*.

While the power of fear gave East Germany's police the ability to invade citizens' privacy—thereby giving the state total control of its citizens' lives and movement—today, in the "free world," our privacy rights are being violated by the power of convenience.

Daily we are being urged, enticed, and encouraged to accept an invasive and ultimately dehumanizing loss of control over the data that is an expression of our personality by using the internet. This convenience gives frightening and unfettered power to the large digital companies and governments with the resources to shape and control the technology that is intruding into every area of our lives. And as these practices continue, and as the world becomes increasingly digitally connected, the line between convenience and coercion becomes all the more indistinct. When technology is abused, it gives governments and digital companies the power to predict our actions, control our choices, and manipulate our future in far-reaching ways.

All the while this is happening, we are complicit in helping governments and digital companies violate our privacy rights. While we may not (yet) have surveillance cameras in our homes, we have their digital equivalent (or worse) in all our appliances. We carry them in our pockets and on our wrists. While we may not be fully living under Big Brother at this time, we have armies of "Little Brothers" with the ability to watch over us through our smart phones, tablets, watches, and computers every second of the day. Thanks to the power of big data, these Little Brothers often provide a better collective knowledge of us than any Big Brother could ever achieve.

Every day we are freely giving away our thoughts, lives, and secrets (or other people's secrets) online via our use of social media, our internet searches, our "likes" on Facebook and Twitter, our emails, our online purchases, our posts on Instagram, and our efforts to get as many viewers as possible to watch us during live streams on digital platforms like YouTube and Periscope. The permutations of this surrender of our inner selves to the rich and the powerful who control our data is terrifying to those who understand what can be done with our digital fingerprints and the vast predictive capacity of big data.

In the digital era anyone can intimidate, harass, and cyberbully another individual with the click of the mouse or by hitting "send," "tweet," "post," or "publish." Strangers and revenge-seekers can incite others, like online trolls, against a person they wish to harm by "doxxing" them. "Doxxing" (which is sometimes spelled "doxing") is derived from the word "docs." It occurs when an individual with a malicious intent abuses digital media to harm another person by collecting their personal information, like their home address and phone number, and publishes it on the internet to induce others to wreak havoc on their lives—or worse. These dangerous online antics don't always stay online but having been spilling over into the real world.

As our chapters showcasing the individual stories of people fighting for human rights in countries such as China, North Korea, Saudi Arabia, and Iran attest, millions of people are currently living in an ever-expanding surveillance state that is committed to depriving its citizens of any privacy that it decides is a threat to the ruling elite.

At the same time, we in the "free world" are also facing a rising and troubling tide of encroaching surveillance and privacy abuses in the name of "convenience" and "security" by corporations and governmental entities, respectively. Governmental invasion of our fundamental right to privacy is being matched by an equally-dangerous invasion of our privacy by the corporate sector. We must guard against both or we will see future generations suffer as a result.

As Professor Cannataci says, "We all know what we do in the bathroom, but we don't leave the door open."

This is the era of the "Net State," where companies that control much of the internet landscape may have resources that dwarf those of traditional pre-digital nation states. Those who profit from this power, either economically or politically, are often fond of making grossly self-serving predictions that human rights such as privacy are anachronistic. Digital companies that wildly profit from "commodifying" your privacy rights (i.e., turning your private information into a commodity that you then trade away merely for access to their platform or website) do not want to lose that easy, lucrative revenue stream.

"Most people don't understand the technology," says Professor Cannataci. "Here's the problem: The legal mechanisms for protecting your human rights, including privacy, were created prior to the digital era." This means that the digital technology that is radically reshaping so much of our society, economy, and collective lives is racing ahead with little or no connection to a rights framework designed to protect the weakest and most vulnerable from those actors whose thirst for power and wealth leave them with little concern for the wellbeing of society as a whole. It's this gap between the capabilities of the technology and making sure that the technology is only used in ways that respect human rights such as privacy that Cannataci is trying to address.

Part of the difficulty is that not every country comes to the problem with the same legal framework. Some countries, including the United States, have an historical reliance on property law concepts when dealing with personal data. To a great degree, US law tends to treat personal data as the property of those entities that can collect the data online. Conversely, European law is now more likely to treat personal data as an extension of the *human person*—an approach that leads to greater protection for individual citizens. After all, if someone collects your health data, your financial data, data on your opinions and habits, data on your friends and relationships, and other elements of your "digital fingerprint," then they effectively have *you*—at least to such a degree that they can predict and even manipulate your views and actions with shocking accuracy.

Worse than 1984

In the digital era, anyone can have their privacy rights violated, stolen, exploited, and misused by hackers. When data is stolen it can then be used fraudulently, published without your permission, held for ransom, used for blackmail, or worse. These threats are particularly dangerous because they can come from so many different sources—disgruntled contractors or competitors; cyber vigilante groups like Anonymous or Crackas With Attitude (CWA); crime syndicates, drug cartels, and gangs; terrorist organizations such as Al-Qaeda and the Islamic State; political opponents; or even foreign governments such as Russia, China, North Korea, and Iran. These countries rank among the worst human rights abusers of their own citizens, so it's not surprising that they would have little regard for the human rights of foreigners.

"The internet was created after the [Berlin] wall came down. While people love the convenience of the internet and their phones," Professor Cannataci said during his interview for this book, "they are generating hundreds of thousands of electronic fingerprints that would not have been generated twenty-five years ago. This is new and something a communist state did not have. But today 90-99 percent of the data is not given. It is 'metadata.' That metadata can really show who you are. Society should be discussing the ways states and corporations are using data. We need to have a proper debate to ensure everyone's privacy rights are protected."

Hacking is a neverending problem and challenge for governments and corporations worldwide—especially those engaged in the digital sphere. While we are constantly being assured that our data is secure, and while the concept of having a secure database may sound well and good, it is an inherent contradiction in terms.

Take for example when the allegedly highly secure United States Office of Personnel Management was hacked in 2015. It was reported that, "approximately 5.6 million digital images of government employee fingerprints" were stolen.[172] Chinese hackers accessed the security clearance applications of nearly twenty million Americans—their fingerprints, their social security numbers, their family members, the names of their friends, neighbors, and foreign contacts, and much more.[173]

In the private sector, "every single Yahoo account was hacked in 2014—three billion in all."[174] In 2015, the credit reporting agency Experian admitted that hackers accessed its systems and stole personal data on fifteen million individuals, to include names, addresses, PIN numbers, passport numbers, and military IDs.[175] These are just a couple of the biggest ones, but these kinds of incidents are occurring all the time—so often, in fact, that they don't get much attention.

In a notoriously embarrassing episode for the US intelligence community, in August 2018, a British teenager was sentenced in London to two years in prison after he broke into former head of the Central Intelligence Agency (CIA) John Brennan's AOL account, former Director of National Intelligence (DNI) James Clappers's internet provider account, and the accounts of several other high-level US government officials. He was fifteen years old and was a part of a hacking group called Crackas With Attitude (CWA).[176] And the list of hacks and data breaches goes on and on.

According to the 2017 Hiscox Readiness Report, which was based upon a survey conducted with 3,000 companies across three countries and assessed their readiness to deal with cybercrime, "The report found 53 percent of the companies assessed were ill-prepared to deal with an attack, and just 30 percent were rated 'expert' in their overall cyber readiness." According to Steve Langan, chief executive at Hiscox Insurance, which put out the report, in 2016 alone:

...cybercrime cost the global economy over $450 billion, over 2 billion personal records were stolen and in the U.S. alone over 100 million Americans had their medical records stolen.... This is an epidemic of cybercrime, and yet 53 percent of businesses in the U.S., U.K. and Germany were just ill-prepared.[177]

Bear in mind that when cybercrime occurs, the companies and agencies that were hacked are not the only victims. So are their insurers, employees, partners, and customers—including police, military, and intelligence personnel; elected officials; and their families.

Anthem, the largest US healthcare insurance provider, for example, recently settled litigation to the tune of $115 million after hackers were able to break into a database in 2015 using a stolen password. The hacked database housed personal information of former and current clients and their employees. Approximately seventy-nine million records were stolen. This included "names, birthdays, social security numbers, addresses, email addresses, and employment and income information."[178]

Imagine the havoc that could be created with the personal data of police, military personnel, and senior government officials if hostile regimes or groups were to hack their mortgage, credit, banking, medical data, or other records. The homes and families of business leaders are also prime targets. If these episodes teach us anything, it is that the term "cybersecurity" is one of the enduring oxymorons of the Digital Age.

Occasionally, there are momentary pauses in the drumbeat of messages urging us to surrender the digital expression of ourselves. They occur when stories of these inevitable abuses surface in the media. But after each such spasmodic episode of public horror at the nightmarish future we are creating for ourselves and our children, we continue down the same path to the future George Orwell warned us about.

As we transition from the advent of the *Digital Age* to the *Internet of Things*, the security risks associated with the unprecedented commerce in personal consumer data will increase exponentially. The more than 8.7 billion devices currently connected to the internet are expected to increase ten-fold within five years. Each such device not only constitutes a point of individual vulnerability, but collectively, they put the security of nations at risk.

Beyond their intended purpose, these devices will also collect and transmit vast amounts of private user data to the manufacturers and other third parties—under the aegis of privacy waivers that are effectively "contracts of adhesion" designed to create a legal fiction of meaningfully consenting to give away one's personal data—all to protect the insatiable corporate appetite for data mining.

Theoretically, citizens are free to protect their privacy by opting out, but in reality, it is simply not possible to do that and still be full participants in the modern economy or society. While these devices provide convenience, the data they transmit can be used in ways that harm individuals and the public more broadly.

For example, although companies can use such information to target their marketing better, others can also use it to screen out potential clients or employees unjustly. While drug stores want to know when your browsing history indicates you might have an ailment for which they have a remedy, health insurers may also want to know that same information so they can alert client companies' human resources departments to avoid hiring prospective employees who might drive up those companies' health care premiums.

We all have a physical body and instinctively understand that external control over our physical person is inherently oppressive and dehumanizing. But what about the nonphysical expression of our person and personality in the form of personal data? As stated earlier, if some powerful actor has access to your health records, your financial data, your personal contacts, your communications, your deeply held beliefs and opinions, your reading and purchasing habits, and a wealth of other personal data…do they not, in a sense, have you? The question becomes particularly disquieting when you consider that the power of big data allows them to create a "digital profile" for you that can predict your views, opinions, voting habits, and other behaviors with a high degree of accuracy.

Since hacking is a permanent feature of life in the Digital Age, the best way to reduce the damage to the public is for corporations to go to data rehab. We need to replace data-binging with moderation. But the personal information of the public has become a form of corporate cocaine for many companies in the era of big data—a drug that is plentiful, highly addictive, and toxic.

So, even when hackers aren't hacking us, we must be concerned that digital companies are selling our private information for personal gain and gratification. Unfortunately, that is precisely what is happening. For example, in April 2018, Facebook confirmed that during the run-up to the United States 2016 Presidential elections, approximately eighty-seven million of their U.S users' information was "improperly" shared with Cambridge Analytica, a political consulting firm in the United Kingdom. As of this writing, investigations into this matter have crossed multiple countries, include the United Kingdom, United States, and Canada, and remain ongoing.

Meanwhile, Cambridge Analytica has since filed for bankruptcy and shut down—and reportedly reopened under a new name.[179]

As Professor Cannataci explained in his interview, "Computer technology is identifying us. By profiling me, you can craft a message to me that is quite different than to the lady next door. That is key in understanding why privacy is so important. It is showing bad actors how to manipulate people into doing what they want."

The harmful, dangerous, and potentially criminal aspects of the internet that are exploited by bad actors make the work of advancing human rights far more difficult. If we do not act to protect our human rights—such as the right to privacy—we will lose them.

Enter Professor Cannataci.

Being a UN Special Rapporteur is not for the faint of heart. Challenging oppressive legal, political, and economic systems can be daunting and frustrating on a good day. The office does not come with a large salary or staff either. Moreover, the forces that one can rile as a Special Rapporteur can be dangerous, considering that invading people's privacy is not only profitable, but holds great power. Those individuals who are invading your privacy do not want to give up their ability to do so and will go to great lengths not to.

One of the additional challenges Cannataci faces while advocating for greater protection of your privacy rights is the fact that nation-states, powerful corporations, and other key actors cannot agree on a simple definition of privacy. True, differences in various cultures play a role. For example, as Professor Cannataci simply explained, "What is considered private in France is not private in Saudi Arabia."

Of course, the text of Article 12 of the Universal Declaration protecting the fundamental right of privacy dates to a pre-digital era. Now, the challenge before us all is to ensure that this vision of a fundamental right of privacy—and all that depends upon it—is not lost for future generations living in the Digital Age.

To understand the stakes in this effort, remember that around the world people are imprisoned, tortured, and killed as a result of the invasion of their privacy. Some also face similar persecution for their defense of privacy and other closely related human rights. In most cases, we will never know the names of these victims. But there are a few frontline heroes whose stories we do know. They embody the tremendous stakes in the global struggle to protect our rights from the forces that visionaries such as Orwell and Professor Cannataci have spent their lives laboring to warn us about.

In Egypt, for instance, Ramy Raoof, who was a part of the Egyptian Initiative for Personal Rights during the 2011 Revolution in Tahrir Square in Cairo, was reportedly beaten up several times. Regarding one of the clashes between citizens and the military, Raoof recounted how "bodies arrived overnight at a nearby hospital.…[I]t was difficult to tell what kind of bullets killed the protesters and…full autopsies were expected."[180]

Today Raoof develops strategies to keep digital data private. He focuses on surveillance patterns, developing privacy protocols, and holistic privacy, and he is a strong advocate for free and open encryption. He was a part of the team with the Citizen Lab in Toronto that exposed a "large scale phishing campaign," called Nile Phish. The targets were Egyptian Non-Governmental Organizations (NGOs).

> Phishing is a tactic to steal personal information, like passwords, through deception. Many phishing emails often try to trick you into entering passwords and other secret codes into websites that look legitimate, but are really fake.

> While phishing can be used by criminal gangs to steal bank information and for other financial crimes, phishing is also used for espionage and surveillance. For example, the Nile Phish operation seems to be designed to gain access to email accounts and document sharing files belonging to NGOs.[181]

The phishing campaign was against Egyptian civil society during the "unprecedented crackdown" during the 2011 revolution, which ultimately led to former president Muhammad Hosni El Sayed Mubarak being ousted from power after serving as Egypt's president for thirty years.

The phishing campaign primarily targeted organizations that support human rights and individuals like lawyers, journalists, and other human rights activists. It tried to steal passwords using bogus emails with familiar language, inviting the email recipients—NGO staffers—to a fictional conference the phishers had also falsely claimed was being supported by other NGOs. From there, the NGO staffers were directed to learn more about the panelists at the conference. "The link led to a site designed to trick the target into believing that they needed to enter their password to view the file."[182]

In an interview with the Argentinian NGO *Centro de Estudios Legales y Sociales* (CELS), Raoof sounded the alarm:

> Privacy is an entry point to all civil liberties and human rights. If you are able to maintain a decent level of privacy, you can freely seek knowledge and share knowledge and produce knowledge. You will be free and able to access medical care and health information and sexual knowledge, you will be able to politically organize, and raise

your kids, and do anything you want to do. Without proper privacy, you cannot take an informed position or give informed consent. If someone is always giving you choices—X or Y, there is no Z, there is no other option—and someone is always deciding on your behalf, you are not really free.[183]

In Mexico, Luis Fernando García, the Executive Director of *Red en Defensa de los Derechos Digitales* (R3D), warns how "surveillance can cost you your life or your liberty."

R3D is a digital rights group. It uses "various legal and communication tools for policy research, strategic litigation, advocacy, and campaigns." With an emphasis on freedom of expression, privacy, and access to knowledge, their mission is to promote digital rights in Mexico.[184] Less than two years since R3D was founded while working with other groups, including Toronto University's The Citizens Lab, SocialTIC and Article 19 Mexico, they have already exposed surveillance abuses in Mexico.

One of their investigations found "Mexican authorities had used NSO Group's Pegasus spyware to target journalists and human rights defenders working to expose government corruption and human rights abuses."

NSO Group is a surveillance technology company that does business exclusively with governments. The attacks on journalists and human rights defenders "were designed to compromise the mobile phones of targeted individuals, permitting the attackers to surreptitiously turn on cameras and microphones, record calls, read messages, and track movements."

In addition, RB3 found this NSO malware was being used not just to spy on journalists, and human rights activists, but for other purposes as well—including for commercial profit.

As García explained in an interview with Access Now, a human rights advocacy group, the sophisticated NSO malware works like this:

Targets received an SMS message that included a link. One message read that the target was highlighted in a negative news story, and included a link to that article. In another instance, a message said that the target's daughter had been in an accident, and the link would reveal where she had been hospitalized. When the target clicked the link, the malware exploited vulnerabilities in the user's iPhone that infected it with NSO Group's malware, which is called Pegasus. Pegasus takes control of the device and allows you to record voice and video, read messages, and know the device's location.

"Your privacy *is* your security," Garcia said. "They're the same thing. People should understand that there are legal safeguards in Mexico, but they don't work. We've shown that 99 percent of government surveillance of metadata occurs without a warrant when the law requires one."[185]

In the increasingly global world of the Digital Age, international cooperation among different states is necessary to help ensure that everyone's privacy rights are protected—not just the rights of *some* people, in *some* places, *some* of the time. This is necessary so that the many heroes of *Human Liberty 2.0*—only a few of whom we have profiled in this book—are able to continue using digital media to advance human rights and for the good of all.

If unchecked, the accelerating abuse of privacy rights in our world could create a human rights nightmare. Indeed, apart from the efforts of Professor Cannataci and other privacy champions like Ramy Raoof and Luis Fernando García, there is little to prevent a substantial portion of the world's population from living under conditions that would have been the East German Stasi police-state's dream. In the pre-digital era, surveillance was labor-intensive. To spy on someone, you had to follow them, tap their phone, break into their house or apartment, open their mail, and so on. Now, the government, powerful digital media corporations, criminal syndicates, and terrorist organizations can spy on millions effortlessly through a vast and growing array of internet-connected devices.

In some parts of our world, such as North Korea and parts of China, Big Brother is already a reality. But even in the free world, Little Brothers are threatening us with an Orwellian future unless we do more to safeguard everyone's fundamental right to privacy.

CHAPTER 26

DIGITAL MEDIA AND FUTURE OF FREEDOM

We have come a long way from the revolution begun by the invention of the printing press to the ongoing revolution of the Digital Age. As we have seen, there are dehumanizing forces of oppression seeking to harness the power of digital technology for evil. But I remain convinced that the most encouraging dimension of the greatest technological revolution of our time is only starting to be felt in our increasingly global culture.

Every day, around the world, new chapters are being written in the ever expanding and far-reaching story of *Human Liberty 2.0*. In spite of the countervailing forces of evil and oppression, the global phenomenon of people harnessing the power of digital and social media for good—in ways that both express and recognize our common humanity—has shown itself to be a force for good that cannot be ignored. While it may seem amorphous in comparison to the organized violence of movements such as ISIS—or the technological edifice of China's Firewall—the growing influence, pervasiveness, and staying power of the global trend that we call *Human Liberty 2.0* derives from our shared human longing for freedom. In this interconnected era, we all need to work for a world that affirms rather than denies the dignity that is the birthright of all members of the human family.

The promotion of human rights and human dignity—and the conditions that allow for both to be fully expressed and realized—unleashes tremendous human, social, and economic potential. For this reason, the advance of *Human Liberty 2.0* is everyone's business. The notion of ordinary people sharing in this great enterprise seemed like a dream in 1948—and for many of the decades since the drafting of the world's most important human rights document. But the media revolution of the Digital Age has closed the gap and empowered anybody and everybody to be able to do something concrete to advance human rights, expose abuses, and help others in peril. To a degree never before true in human history, the future of freedom is in our hands.

As we have seen in stories that have taken us from Seattle to Ethiopia to Haiti and beyond, no longer do we necessarily need to wait for governments or international organizations to take the lead when a crisis erupts, emergencies break out, or people are being oppressed. This is very important since these traditional manifestations of a centralized, bureaucratic authority model have repeatedly demonstrated their own serious failings in these areas.

This spectacular opportunity aligns with other well-known examples of positive digital media disruptions, including in commerce, politics, media, and education. Although we are at an early stage in the process, the internet may also be beginning to disrupt the notion that large bureaucracies such as government agencies or the United Nations can and should be the exclusive or even primary global guardian of human rights. If so, then the internet is definitely helping to make the vision of the drafters of the Universal Declaration a reality in our time. As the people have increasingly become the press, so too can (and should) they see themselves as increasingly becoming human rights guardians in the Digital Age.

Consider what this means for all of us.

Today, tomorrow, and beyond, everyone can engage in order to raise awareness and promote human dignity in ways that were never possible in the pre-digital world. Today's digital good Samaritans can collaborate with others of goodwill—locally and internationally—to help advance human dignity and flourishing at home or around the world.

What will you do?

Edmund Burke, the Irish statesman, political thinker, and author of "Reflections on the Revolution in France" that was published in 1790, once said, "The only thing necessary for the triumph of evil is for good men to do nothing."[186] Burke's insightful words have withstood the test of time and are as relevant today as they were when he first wrote them.

CHAPTER 27

JOIN THE HUMAN LIBERTY 2.0 REVOLUTION

In spite of the violence and horror so often featured in the news media, this book series tells one of the most inspiring stories of our time—a story that is happening all around us.

Although we may not realize it, we are living through a revolutionary moment in the history of human liberty that is happening everywhere the internet can reach. The growth of the World Wide Web and increasing global support for the concept of universal rights have converged to create opportunities for almost anyone with internet access to contribute to the cause of human freedom. The opportunities to be a digital good Samaritan have never been greater.

With the rapid global spread of digital and social media, people are reaching out across geographical and cultural boundaries to advance universal rights, resist oppression, and promote the dignity of all human beings. If you have read even a few of the stories in this book series, you will be aware of some of the many ways in which technologies such as digital video, social media, and crowdmapping are helping ordinary people to challenge oppression, share information, and extend a hand of compassion to others. These are not just a few isolated incidents but a broad trend that offers hope for a greater shared commitment to the dream of universal human rights.

With the rise of a generation shaped by the social and cultural changes of the Digital Age, we now have the power to push the collective pursuit of human liberty and human compassion into the smallest crevices of the world, one person at a time. The real story of *Human Liberty 2.0* is only just beginning. Become a part of it!

"GO AND DO LIKEWISE"

"Go and do likewise" is the closing admonition to the famous parable of the Good Samaritan who reached out across boundaries of race and religion to help someone in desperate need.

Anyone reading this book has already raised their hand as someone who cares about the fundamental rights of others. So, we encourage you to draw inspiration from the real-life examples in this book and find ways to use your own unique talents and abilities to help advance the cause of *Human Liberty 2.0* in our world.

To help you find ways to engage, we have listed below some of the many organizations whose work is featured in this book:

Charity: water: www.charitywater.org

Crisis Mappers Net: www.crisismappers.net

Exchange Initiative: www.exchangeinitiative.com/traffickcam

Flash Drives for Freedom: flashdrivesforfreedom.org

FoodCloud: https://food.cloud

Humans of New York: www.humansofnewyork.com

My Stealthy Freedom: www.facebook.com/StealthyFreedom

National Center for Missing and Exploited Children: www.missingkids.com

Nothing But Nets: nothingbutnets.net

Polaris: polarisproject.org

Reporters Without Borders: rsf.org/en

SocialBlood: www.facebook.com/socialblood

United for Iran: united4iran.org/en/

Ushahidi: www.ushahidi.com

THE UNIVERSAL DECLARATION OF HUMAN RIGHTS (UNITED NATIONS 1948)

Preamble

Whereas recognition of the inherent dignity and of the equal and inalienable rights of all members of the human family is the foundation of freedom, justice and peace in the world,

Whereas disregard and contempt for human rights have resulted in barbarous acts which have outraged the conscience of mankind, and the advent of a world in which human beings shall enjoy freedom of speech and belief and freedom from fear and want has been proclaimed as the highest aspiration of the common people,

Whereas it is essential, if man is not to be compelled to have recourse, as a last resort, to rebellion against tyranny and oppression, that human rights should be protected by the rule of law,

Whereas it is essential to promote the development of friendly relations between nations,

Whereas the peoples of the United Nations have in the Charter reaffirmed their faith in fundamental human rights, in the dignity and worth of the human person and in the equal rights of men and women and have determined to promote social progress and better standards of life in larger freedom,

Whereas Member States have pledged themselves to achieve, in co-operation with the United Nations, the promotion of universal respect for and observance of human rights and fundamental freedoms,

Whereas a common understanding of these rights and freedoms is of the greatest importance for the full realization of this pledge,

Now, Therefore THE GENERAL ASSEMBLY proclaims THIS UNIVERSAL DECLARATION OF HUMAN RIGHTS as a common standard of achievement for all peoples and all nations, to the end that every individual and every organ of society, keeping this Declaration constantly in mind, shall strive by teaching and education to promote respect for these rights and freedoms and by progressive measures, national and international, to secure their universal and effective recognition and observance, both among the peoples of Member States themselves and among the peoples of territories under their jurisdiction.

Article 1:

All human beings are born free and equal in dignity and rights. They are endowed with reason and conscience and should act towards one another in a spirit of brotherhood.

Article 2:

Everyone is entitled to all the rights and freedoms set forth in this Declaration, without distinction of any kind, such as race, colour, sex, language, religion, political or other opinion, national or social origin, property, birth or other status. Furthermore, no distinction shall be made on the basis of the political, jurisdictional or international status of the country or territory to which a person belongs, whether it be independent, trust, non-self-governing or under any other limitation of sovereignty.

Article 3:

Everyone has the right to life, liberty and security of person.

Article 4:

No one shall be held in slavery or servitude; slavery and the slave trade shall be prohibited in all their forms.

Article 5:

No one shall be subjected to torture or to cruel, inhuman or degrading treatment or punishment.

Article 6:

Everyone has the right to recognition everywhere as a person before the law.

Article 7:

All are equal before the law and are entitled without any discrimination to equal protection of the law. All are entitled to equal protection against any discrimination in violation of this Declaration and against any incitement to such discrimination.

Article 8:

Everyone has the right to an effective remedy by the competent national tribunals for acts violating the fundamental rights granted him by the constitution or by law.

Article 9:

No one shall be subjected to arbitrary arrest, detention or exile.

Article 10:

Everyone is entitled in full equality to a fair and public hearing by an independent and impartial tribunal, in the determination of his rights and obligations and of any criminal charge against him.

Article 11:

(1) Everyone charged with a penal offence has the right to be presumed innocent until proved guilty according to law in a public trial at which he has had all the guarantees necessary for his defence.

(2) No one shall be held guilty of any penal offence on account of any act or omission which did not constitute a penal offence, under national or international law, at the time when it was committed. Nor shall a heavier penalty be imposed than the one that was applicable at the time the penal offence was committed.

Article 12:

No one shall be subjected to arbitrary interference with his privacy, family, home or correspondence, nor to attacks upon his honour and reputation. Everyone has the right to the protection of the law against such interference or attacks.

Article 13:

(1) Everyone has the right to freedom of movement and residence within the borders of each state.

(2) Everyone has the right to leave any country, including his own, and to return to his country.

Article 14:

(1) Everyone has the right to seek and to enjoy in other countries asylum from persecution.

(2) This right may not be invoked in the case of prosecutions genuinely arising from non-political crimes or from acts contrary to the purposes and principles of the United Nations.

Article 15:

(1) Everyone has the right to a nationality.

(2) No one shall be arbitrarily deprived of his nationality nor denied the right to change his nationality.

Article 16:

(1) Men and women of full age, without any limitation due to race, nationality or religion, have the right to marry and to found a family. They are entitled to equal rights as to marriage, during marriage and at its dissolution.

(2) Marriage shall be entered into only with the free and full consent of the intending spouses.(3) The family is the natural and fundamental group unit of society and is entitled to protection by society and the State.

Article 17:

(1) Everyone has the right to own property alone as well as in association with others.

(2) No one shall be arbitrarily deprived of his property.

Article 18:

Everyone has the right to freedom of thought, conscience and religion; this right includes freedom to change his religion or belief, and freedom, either alone or in community with others and in public or private, to manifest his religion or belief in teaching, practice, worship and observance.

Article 19:

Everyone has the right to freedom of opinion and expression; this right includes freedom to hold opinions without interference and to seek, receive and impart information and ideas through any media and regardless of frontiers.

Article 20:

(1) Everyone has the right to freedom of peaceful assembly and association.

(2) No one may be compelled to belong to an association.

Article 21:

(1) Everyone has the right to take part in the government of his country, directly or through freely chosen representatives.

(2) Everyone has the right of equal access to public service in his country.

(3) The will of the people shall be the basis of the authority of government; this will shall be expressed in periodic and genuine elections which shall be by universal and equal suffrage and shall be held by secret vote or by equivalent free voting procedures.

Article 22:

Everyone, as a member of society, has the right to social security and is entitled to realization, through national effort and international co-operation and in accordance with the organization and resources of each State, of the economic, social and cultural rights indispensable for his dignity and the free development of his personality.

Article 23:

(1) Everyone has the right to work, to free choice of employment, to just and favourable conditions of work and to protection against unemployment.

(2) Everyone, without any discrimination, has the right to equal pay for equal work.

(3) Everyone who works has the right to just and favourable remuneration ensuring for himself and his family an existence worthy of human dignity, and supplemented, if necessary, by other means of social protection.

(4) Everyone has the right to form and to join trade unions for the protection of his interests.

Article 24:

Everyone has the right to rest and leisure, including reasonable limitation of working hours and periodic holidays with pay.

Article 25:

(1) Everyone has the right to a standard of living adequate for the health and well-being of himself and of his family, including food, clothing, housing and medical care and necessary social services, and the right to security in the event of unemployment, sickness, disability, widowhood, old age or other lack of livelihood in circumstances beyond his control.

(2) Motherhood and childhood are entitled to special care and assistance. All children, whether born in or out of wedlock, shall enjoy the same social protection.

Article 26:

(1) Everyone has the right to education. Education shall be free, at least in the elementary and fundamental stages. Elementary education shall be compulsory. Technical and professional education shall be made generally available and higher education shall be equally accessible to all on the basis of merit.

(2) Education shall be directed to the full development of the human personality and to the strengthening of respect for human rights and fundamental freedoms. It shall promote understanding, tolerance and friendship among all nations, racial or religious groups, and shall further the activities of the United Nations for the maintenance of peace.

(3) Parents have a prior right to choose the kind of education that shall be given to their children.

Article 27:

(1) Everyone has the right freely to participate in the cultural life of the community, to enjoy the arts and to share in scientific advancement and its benefits.

(2) Everyone has the right to the protection of the moral and material interests resulting from any scientific, literary or artistic production of which he is the author.

Article 28:

Everyone is entitled to a social and international order in which the rights and freedoms set forth in this Declaration can be fully realized.

Article 29:

(1) Everyone has duties to the community in which alone the free and full development of his personality is possible.

(2) In the exercise of his rights and freedoms, everyone shall be subject only to such limitations as are determined by law solely for the purpose of securing due recognition and respect for the rights and freedoms of others and of meeting the just requirements of morality, public order and the general welfare in a democratic society.

(3) These rights and freedoms may in no case be exercised contrary to the purposes and principles of the United Nations.

Article 30:

Nothing in this Declaration may be interpreted as implying for any State, group or person any right to engage in any activity or to perform any act aimed at the destruction of any of the rights and freedoms set forth herein.[187]

ACKNOWLEDGMENTS

The author is indebted to many human rights experts—both scholars and practitioners—as well as others whose advice, insights, and example were formative to the creation of this book.

As a scholar and a friend, Professor Mary Ann Glendon of Harvard Law School has influenced the author's education and involvement in the field of law and human rights for over two decades. Professor Joe Cannataci, the UN Special Rapporteur for Privacy, has been an example of tireless human rights leadership by a public intellectual faced with a daunting global mandate.

In the United Kingdom, the author is especially indebted Lord David Alton of Liverpool, Nazir Afzal OBE, and Lord Michael Hastings of Scarisbrick for their advice and example of a life of service to the marginalized. The author also wishes to thank Dean Abimbola Olowofoyeku and Professor Ben Chigara of Brunel Law School, London, for their steadfast support.

In South Korea, the author is indebted to Professor Park Sun Young of Dongguk University, Professor Seong-Phil Hong of Yonsei University, and Martin Uden, former British ambassador to the Republic of Korea, for educating him on the human rights atrocities of the North Korean regime.

In the United States, Ambassador Andrew Young's support and service to the cause of civil and human rights has been both an example and an inspiration. The author is also indebted to the Honorable Toney Collins, Dr. Rita Jackson Samuels, and other members of the Board of the Martin Luther King Jr. Advisory Council of the State of Georgia whose gracious support has been a tremendous encouragement.

The launch of this book series was made possible through the gracious encouragement and editorial support of Anthony Ziccardi and Nikki Sinning at Post Hill Press as well as the intrepid efforts of Teresa Hartnett of the Hartnett Literary Agency.

Finally, the author also wishes to thank Sahar Shah and Albert Gombis whose contributions in editing this book were invaluable.

ENDNOTES

1. The Warsaw Ghetto Uprising occurred in 1943, when Jewish resistance fighters, in German-occupied Poland, revolted and fought against the German military. See "Warsaw Ghetto Uprising," *The History Channel*. http://www.history.com/topics/world-war-ii/warsaw-ghetto-uprising

2. The North Korean regime practices a particularly brutal form of collective punishment such that when one individual commits an offense, the punishment is meted out against that person's entire family; the offender's parents, spouse, and children can be imprisoned, tortured, and executed. As a result, children born in the prison camps can spend their entire lives there. *See*: http://www.northkoreanow.org/the-crisis/north-koreas-gulags/

3. Claire Breay, Julian Harrison, "Magna Carta: an introduction," *British Library*. http://www.bl.uk/magna-carta/articles/magna-carta-an-introduction

4. There is deep irony in the fact that the China created the original elements of print media and now is the global leader in technology designed to censor and suppress digital media.

5. First Lady of the United States and wife of Franklin D. Roosevelt who played a decisive role in the process that led to the successful drafting of the Universal Declaration of Human Rights.

6. Eleanor Roosevelt, "1958 speech delivered on the tenth anniversary of the Universal Declaration of Human Rights," *United Nations*. http://www.un.org/en/globalissues/briefingpapers/humanrights/quotes.shtml.

7. Most statements of rights throughout history have been addressed to monarchs or governments. For example, in the American context, the Declaration of Independence was addressed to the King of England.

8. 1994: Rwanda presidents' plane 'shot down,' *BBC*, April 6, 1994. http://news.bbc.co.uk/onthisday/hi/dates/stories/april/6/newsid_2472000/2472195.stm. Also see: "Report: Rebels cleared in

plane crash that sparked Rwandan genocide," *CNN,* January 11, 2012. http://www.cnn.com/2012/01/11/world/africa/rwanda-president-plane/.

9   Terry J. Allen, "The General and the Genocide," *Amnesty International Magazine.* http://www.terryjallen.com/journo-subP/dallaire.htm.

10   President Bill Clinton, "Text of Clinton's Rwanda Speech," *White House,* March 25, 1998. http://www.cbsnews.com/news/text-of-clintons-rwanda-speech/

11   Christopher Rhoads and Geoffrey A. Fowler, "Egypt Shuts Down Internet, Cell phone Services," *Wall Street Journal,* January 29, 2011. http://www.wsj.com/articles/SB10001424052748703956604576110453371369740

12   Jeffrey Gettleman, "Disputed vote plunges Kenya into Bloodshed," *New York Times*, December 31, 2007. http://www.nytimes.com/2007/12/31/world/africa/31kenya.html?pagewanted=all&_r=0

13   "Kenyans burned to death in church,"*BBC News*, January 1, 2008. http://news.bbc.co.uk/2/hi/7166932.stm

14   Ushahidi. http://www.ushahidi.com/

15   "Haiti Earthquake Fast Facts," *CNN,* January 6, 2015. http://www.cnn.com/2013/12/12/world/haiti-earthquake-fast-facts/

16   Patrick Meier and Chrissy Martin, "Ushahidi Haiti Project Evaluation," *Ushahidi.com.* http://www.ushahidi.com/2011/04/19/ushahidi-haiti-project-evaluation-final-report/

17   "'Ushahidi' Technology Saves Lives in Haiti and Chile," *Newsweek,* March 3, 2010. http://www.newsweek.com/ushahidi-technology-saves-lives-haiti-and-chile-210262

18   Patrick Meier's biography. https://irevolutions.org/bio/.

19   Crisis Mappers Network. www.crisismappers.net/

20   Reporters Without Borders: http://en.rsf.org/

21   Reporters Without Borders Press Freedom Barometer, *Reporters Without Borders*: http://en.rsf.org/press-freedom-barometer-journalists-killed.html

22   "Your Majesty, Don't Let Raef Badawi Be Lashed 1,000 Times!" *Reporters Without Borders Online Petition.* https://rsf.org/petitions/badawi/petition.php?lang=en

23 "Free Raif Badawi" Facebook page. https://www.facebook.com/free.
badawi/

24 "Moscow court gives Ukrainian journalist 12 years for 'spying,'"
Reporters Without Borders, June 6, 2018. https://rsf.org/en/news/
moscow-court-gives-ukrainian-journalist-12-years-spying. *See also:*
"Roman Sushchenko Imprisoned," Committee to Protect Journalists,
September 30, 2016. https://cpj.org/data/people/roman-sushchenko/

25 *See also:* "Iran blogger jailed for 19 years," *Associated Press*,
September 28, 2010. http://www.theguardian.com/world/2010/sep/28/
iran-blogger-jailed-19-years-hossain-derakhshan

26 Akbar Ganji, "Iran's Green Movement five years later – 'Defeated'
but ultimately victorious," *Huffington Post,* June 9, 2014. http://
www.huffingtonpost.com/akbar-ganji/iran-green-movement-five-
years_b_5470078.html

27 Simon Jeffery, "Iran Election protests: the dead, jailed and missing," *The
Guardian,* July 29, 2009. http://www.theguardian.com/world/blog/2009/
jul/29/iran-election-protest-dead-missing

28 "Revolutionary Guards target Internet activists," *Reporters Without
Borders*, June 22, 2015. http://en.rsf.org/iran-revolutionary-guards-
target-22-06-2015,48020.html

29 "For defending press freedom in Iran: 1,000 days in prison and
counting," *Reporters Without Borders,* January 30, 2018. https://rsf.org/
en/news/defending-press-freedom-iran-1000-days-prison-and-counting

30 "Prominent Iranian female prison has forgotten how her twin children
look like," *Al Alrabiya English,* December 2017. http://english.alarabiya.
net/en/features/2017/12/04/Prominent-Iranian-female-prisoner-has-
forgotten-how-her-children-look-like-.html

31 Reporters Without Borders 2018 World Press Freedom Index, *Reporters
Without Borders.* https://rsf.org/en/ranking_table

32 *Azadi: Songs of Freedom of Iran.* http://azadimusic.bandcamp.com/

33 Listen: "Die for My People," http://azadimusic.bandcamp.com/track/
revolution-of-the-mind-die-for-my-people; "Darkest Light" http://
azadimusic.bandcamp.com/track/ayla-nereo-darkest-light; "Freedom

Glory Be Our Name," http://azadimusic.bandcamp.com/track/johnny-b-azari-freedom-glory-be-our-name.

34   *TED: Where Technology, Entertainment and Design converged.* https://www.ted.com/

35   Manal al-Sharif's *TED talk,* June 2013. https://www.ted.com/speakers/manal_al_sharif

36   Manal al-Sharif, "A brief drive in Saudi Arabia changed my life," *The Atlantic,* June 23, 2018. Adapted from Manal al-Sharif's book, *Daring to Drive: A Saudi Woman's Awakening.* https://www.theatlantic.com/international/archive/2018/06/saudi-arabia-women-driving-ban/562784/

37   Manal al-Sharif on *YouTube.* https://www.youtube.com/watch?feature=player_embedded&v=BT-3I5jg1xg

38   *Also see* for comprehensive coverage, Second Update on Manal Al-Sharif, *Saudi woman's Weblog,* May 26, 2011. http://saudiwoman.me/2011/05/26/second-update-on-manal-al-sherif/

39   Rosa Parks was a soft-spoken elderly woman and civil rights pioneer who ignited the boycott of segregated public facilities in Montgomery, Alabama, known as the Montgomery Bus Boycott. Ambassador Andrew Young and other civil rights leaders widely credit Parks with inspiring a generation of younger activist who felt challenged by her courageous example of resistance to racial apartheid in the American South

40   Dr. King's brilliant rebuttal to similar accusations is contained in his famous *Letter from a Birmingham Jail.* To other clergy publicly accusing him of criminal activity for disturbing the public order, he wrote: *"In your statement you assert that our actions, even though peaceful, must be condemned because they precipitate violence. But is this a logical assertion? Isn't this like condemning a robbed man because his possession of money precipitated the evil act of robbery?"*

41   Alaa Wardi, "No woman, no drive." https://www.youtube.com/watch?v=aZMbTFNp4wI

42   Martin Chulov, Nadia al-Faour in Jeddah, "'I feel free like a bird': Saudi women celebrate as driving ban lifted," *The Guardian,* June 24, 2018. https://www.theguardian.com/world/2018/jun/24/saudi-arabia-women-celebrate-as-driving-ban-lifted

43   Prince Alwaleed bin Talal's Media Office Handout, June 24, 2018, *The Guardian.* https://www.theguardian.com/world/video/2018/jun/24/saudi-prince-alwaleed-driven-by-daughter-as-driving-ban-lifted-video

44   Manal al-Sharif, "A brief drive in Saudi Arabia changed my life," *The Atlantic*, June 23, 2018. Adapted from Manal al-Sharif's book, *Daring to Drive: A Saudi Woman's Awakening.* https://www.theatlantic.com/international/archive/2018/06/saudi-arabia-women-driving-ban/562784/

45   Manal Al-Sharif's Web site. http://manal-alsharif.com/

46   "Iranians outraged over arrest of teenager for Instagram dancing clips," *Reuters,* July 9, 2018. https://www.reuters.com/article/us-iran-arrest-instagram/iranians-outraged-over-arrest-of-teenage-for-instagram-dancing-clips-idUSKBN1JZ1VI

47   #DancingIsNotaCrime at Twitter. https://twitter.com/search?q=%23dancingisnotacrime&f=videos&src=tyah. *See also* on Instagram: https://www.instagram.com/explore/tags/dancingisnotacrime/?hl=en

48   "Iranians outraged over arrest of teenager for Instagram dancing clips," *Reuters,* July 9, 2018. https://www.reuters.com/article/us-iran-arrest-instagram/iranians-outraged-over-arrest-of-teenage-for-instagram-dancing-clips-idUSKBN1JZ1VI

49   Masih Alinejab interview with Tina Brown, "How Masih Alinejad started a social movement against forced hijab," *Women in the World*, April 7, 2016. https://www.youtube.com/watch?v=w4B0RGWpudo

50   My Stealthy Freedom Facebook page. https://www.facebook.com/StealthyFreedom/photos/a.859102224103873.1073741828.858832800797482/1070691802944913/?type=1

51   Saeed Kamali Dehghan, "Iranian woman wins rights award for hijab campaign," *The Guardian*, February 24, 2015.https://www.theguardian.com/world/2015/feb/24/iranian-woman-wins-rights-award-hijab-campaign

52   Saeed Kamali Dehghan, "Iranian woman wins rights award for hijab campaign," *The Guardian*, February 24, 2015. https://www.theguardian.com/world/2015/feb/24/iranian-woman-wins-rights-award-hijab-campaign

53   Erin Cunningham, "Women in Iran are pulling off their headscarves—and hoping for a 'turning point.'" *Washington Post,* March 8 2018. https://www.washingtonpost.com/world/women-in-iran-are-pulling-off-their-headscarves--and-hoping-for-a-turning-point/2018/03/08/bb238a96-217c-11e8-946c-9420060cb7bd_story.html?noredirect=on&utm_term=.7e96756cc2a9

54   Robin Wright, "Hijab Protests Expose Iran's Core Divide," *New Yorker,* February 7, 2018. https://www.newyorker.com/news/news-desk/hijab-protests-expose-irans-core-divide

55   Mashih Alinejad, *The Wind in My Hair: My Fight for Freedom in Modern Iran,* (Little Brown and Company, May 29, 2018). https://www.amazon.com/Wind-My-Hair-Freedom-Modern/dp/031654891X

56   Sarah Dean, "The woman Iran can't silence: Jailed as a teen, sentenced to 74 lashes and finally forced into exile, now she's helping millions of women fight against being forced to wear the hijab," UK *Daily Mail,* June 7, 2018. http://www.dailymail.co.uk/news/article-5807353/Masih-Alinejad-says-Iranian-regime-holding-women-hostage-hijab.html

57   Saeed Kamail Dehgham, "Tehran hijab protest: Iranian police arrest 29 women," *The Guardian,* February 2, 2018. https://www.theguardian.com/world/2018/feb/02/tehran-hijab-protest-iranian-police-arrest-29-women

58   "Turning Facebook into the World's Largest Blood Bank," *TedX Talks,* February 6, 2013. https://www.youtube.com/watch?v=l1t3t1OXsHg. *See also*, for example: "Speech of Dr. Juliet Fleischl for World Blood Day, WHO Representative to the LAO People's Democratic Republic," *World Health Organization*, June 14, 2017. http://www.wpro.who.int/laos/mediacentre/speeches/2017/20170614-WBDD-2017/en/

59   "Blood Needs & Blood Supply," *Red Cross.* https://www.redcrossblood.org/donate-blood/how-to-donate/how-blood-donations-help/blood-needs-blood-supply.html

60   "Blood Needs & Blood Supply," *American Red Cross.* https://www.redcrossblood.org/donate-blood/

61   "Listen to Your Users More than Your Competition": Karthik Naralasetty, Founder, SocialBlood, *The Economist,* March 12, 2015. https://health.

economictimes.indiatimes.com/news/industry/listen-to-your-users-ur-competition-karthik-naralasetty-founder-socialblood/46529359

62   "SocialBlood at Facebook," *Facebook Global Marketing Conference 2013,* May 23, 2013. https://www.youtube.com/watch?v=nAv6kuj82IU

63   Shabana Hussain, "Blood ties: Karthik Naralasetty, saving lives by finding donors," *Forbes,* February 19, 2015. http://www.forbesindia.com/article/30-under-30/blood-ties-karthik-naralasetty-saving-lives-by-finding-donors/39589/1

64   SocialBlood's #BleedHope campaign. https://www.facebook.com/socialblood/videos/891684790919812/

65   "Turning Facebook into the world's largest blood bank: Karthik Naralasetty," *Tedx Talks,* February 6, 2013. https://www.youtube.com/watch?v=l1t3t10XsHg

66   Locks of Love. http://www.locksoflove.org/

67   Charity: water. http://www.charitywater.org/

68   Rachel's fundraiser. https://my.charitywater.org/98a87132-a258-4c77-b768-5be1d53e800b/rachels9thbirthday

69   Nicholas Kristof, "Rachel's Last Fund-Raiser," *New York Times,* August 10, 20122. http://www.nytimes.com/2011/08/11/opinion/rachels-last-fund-raiser.html?_r=0

70   "Water Cooperation," *2013 International Year of Water*, Resolution A/RES/65/155. http://www.unwater.org/water-cooperation-2013/water-cooperation/en/

71   Scott Harrison. Meet the Founder of charity: water, *charitywater.org.* http://www.charitywater.org/about/scotts_story.php

72   Mick Krever, "Defected North Korean diplomat: I was a 'modern slave,'" *CNN,* Updated November 3, 2017. https://www.cnn.com/2017/11/02/world/north-korea-defector-thae-yong-ho-amanpour/index.html

73   History.com staff, "Korean war," History.com. 2009. Last accessed June 30, 2018. https://www.history.com/topics/korean-war

74   "Beyond Nuclear Diplomacy: A Regime Insider's Look at North Korea," *Center for Strategic & International Studies,* October 31, 2017.https://www.csis.org/analysis/beyond-nuclear-diplomacy-regime-insiders-look-north-korea

75 Tom Murphy, "Infiltrating North Korea, one USB drive at a time," *CBC News, The National*, February 23, 2018. https://www.youtube.com/watch?v=jKINA-ikgE4

76 About Flashdrivesforfreedom.org. https://flashdrivesforfreedom.org/#about

77 Dalhousie IDS Department and Atlantic Council for International Cooperation, "Jung Gwang-Il Speaks: One Man's Quest to Bring Ideas into North Korea," *Facebook,* January 31, 2018. https://www.facebook.com/events/1333641606781085/

78 Kelly Kasulis, "I spent a day with North Korean defectors, who lived through hell and want a revolution," *Mic Network,* December 22, 2017. https://mic.com/articles/186655/i-spent-a-day-with-north-korean-defectors-who-lived-through-hell-and-want-a-revolution#.t5AhGc6Zp

79 Jung Gwang-il, "Freeing North Korea with flash drives," *Oslo Freedom Forum YouTube*, June 28, 2016. https://www.youtube.com/watch?v=InhKDVUm6Ww

80 Kelly Kasulis, "I spent a day with North Korean defectors, who lived through hell and want a revolution," *Mic.com,* December 22, 2017. https://mic.com/articles/186655/i-spent-a-day-with-north-korean-defectorswho-lived-through-hell-and-want-a-revolution#.jvbkKCAcA

81 Madison Park, "Drones drop films, information into North Korea, activists, say," *CNN,* May 26, 2016. https://www.cnn.com/2016/05/25/asia/north-korea-drones/index.html

82 Jane Onyanga-Omara, "North Korea 'aggressively' jamming new BBC news service: report," *USA Today,* September 27, 2017. https://www.usatoday.com/story/news/world/2017/09/27/north-korea-jamming-bbc-radio-service-report/707342001/

83 Clemente Garavito, Robert Louis Gilmore, Harvey F Kline, James J. Parsons, William Paul McGreevy and The Editors of Encyclopedia Britannica, "Colombia," *Encyclopedia Britannica, June 26, 2018. https://www.britannica.com/place/Colombia/La-Violencia-dictatorship-and-democratic-restoration#ref672067*

84 The Editors of Encyclopedia Britannica, "FARC," *Encyclopedia Britannica*, August 16, 2017. https://www.britannica.com/topic/FARC

85   Simon Romero, "Boy Born to Rebel Hostage Shocks War-Weary Colombia," *New York Times,* June 3, 2007. https://www.nytimes.com/2007/06/03/world/americas/03colombia.html

86   "David D. Burstein, "Innovation Agents: Oscar Morales And One Million Voices Against FARC," *Fast Company,* May 21, 2012. https://www.fastcompany.com/1836318/innovation-agents-oscar-morales-and-one-million-voices-against-farc

87   Maria Camila Perez, "Facebook brings protests to Colombia," *New York Times,* February 8, 2008. https://www.nytimes.com/2008/02/08/business/worldbusiness/08iht-protest11.html

88   "Emancipation Proclamation," *Collected Works of Abraham Lincoln.* http://www.abrahamlincolnonline.org/lincoln/speeches/emancipate.htm

89   "Trafficking in Persons Report," *State Department,* June 2017. https://www.state.gov/j/tip/rls/tiprpt/

90   Rachel Schartz, "Trafficking in Persons Report: 15 Years Later," *Harvard Political Review,* March 16, 2017. http://harvardpolitics.com/world/trafficking-in-persons-report/

91   Nancy Cambria, "A New App Created in St. Louis Aims to Track Down Pimps and Victims of Sex Trafficking," *St. Louis Post-Dispatch,* June 22, 2016, https://www.stltoday.com/news/local/crime-and-courts/a-new-app-created-in-st-louis-aims-to-track/article_984efb3b-8ee1-5f98-94d7-96afeefa5af0.html, "Proud to Serve—Sergeant Adam Kavanaugh," FOX 2 (KTVI: St. Louis), July 27, 2018, https://fox2now.com/2018/07/31/proud-to-serve-adam-kavanaugh/?fbclid=IwAR0D5T66owU9X9ouIU VnWz5_WxqOI-Pm6dyn_VY9I0i1Fxs39uol7PkEoiQ

92   Items 1 through 6 are quoted directly from "Tourism Child-Protection Code of Conduct," ECPAT-USA, https://www.ecpatusa.org/code.

93   "Developing TraffickCam: Inside the Research," Washington University in St. Louis, YouTube, September 1, 2016, https://www.youtube.com/watch?v=zhfHOR6yc98&feature=youtu.be.

94   "Developing TraffickCam: Inside the Research," https://www.youtube.com/watch?v=zhfHOR6yc98&feature=youtu.be.

95 "Developing TraffickCam: Inside the Research," https://www.youtube. com/watch?v=zhfHOR6yc98&feature=youtu.be.

96 Nancy Cambria, "A New App," https://www.stltoday.com/news/ local/crime-and-courts/a-new-app-created-in-st-louis-aims-to-track/ article_984efb3b-8ee1-5f98-94d7-96afeefa5af0.html.

97 "Press Release: Travelers Use TraffickCam App to Fight Sex Trafficking by Uploading Hotel Room Photos to National Database," Exchange Initiative, http://www.exchangeinitiative.com/902-2/.

98 Nancy Cambria, "A New App," https://www.stltoday.com/news/ local/crime-and-courts/a-new-app-created-in-st-louis-aims-to-track/ article_984efb3b-8ee1-5f98-94d7-96afeefa5af0.html.

99 Anna Iovine, "The Dark Reason Why You Should Always Take Pictures of Your Hotel Room," AOL.com, June 23, 2016, https://www.aol.com/ article/news/2016/06/23/the-dark-reason-why-you-should-always-take-pictures-of-your-hote/21400643/.

100 Jacob Long, "App Created to Fight Human Trafficking," 5 On Your Side (KSDK: St. Louis), June 22, 2016, https://www.ksdk.com/article/news/ local/app-created-to-fight-human-trafficking/63-253188670.

101 "Press Release: Travelers Use TraffickCam App to Fight Sex Trafficking by Uploading Hotel Room Photos to National Database," Exchange Initiative, http://www.exchangeinitiative.com/902-2/.

102 "Press Release: Travelers Use TraffickCam App to Fight Sex Trafficking by Uploading Hotel Room Photos to National Database," Exchange Initiative, http://www.exchangeinitiative.com/902-2/.

103 Katy Scott, "Your Hotel Room Photos Could Help Catch Sex Traffickers," CNN.com, March 20, 2017, https://www.cnn. com/2017/02/09/tech/traffickcam-sex-trafficking/index.html.

104 Katy Scott, "Your Hotel Room Photos Could Help Catch Sex Traffickers," https://www.cnn.com/2017/02/09/tech/traffickcam-sex-trafficking/index.html.

105 Anna Iovine, "The Dark Reason Why You Should Always Take Pictures of Your Hotel Room," https://www.aol.com/article/news/2016/06/23/ the-dark-reason-why-you-should-always-take-pictures-of-your-hote/21400643/.

106   Radio interview with Meredith Dank by Jon Lewis, "Study: Atlanta Tops List for Sex Trafficking," *WSB News*. http://patch.com/georgia/buckhead/atlanta-ranked-no-1-for-sex-trafficking-conventions-to-blame. Also see Meredith Dank, et al, "Estimating the Size and Structure of the Underground Commercial Sex Economy in Eight Major US Cities," *The Urban Institute*, March 12, 2014. http://www.urban.org/publications/413047.html

107   "Feds seize Backpage.com, websites in enforcement action," *Associated Press,* April 7, 2018. https://apnews.com/b1770d88ae144ee199ce8403acf10a21?utm_campaign=SocialFlow&utm_source=Twitter&utm_medium=AP

108   "Backpage's Co-founder and CEO, As Well As Several Backpage-Related Corporate Entities, Enter Guilty Pleas," *United States Department of Justice Press Relea*se, April 12, 2018. https://www.justice.gov/opa/pr/backpage-s-co-founder-and-ceo-well-several-backpage-related-corporate-entities-enter-guilty

109   "New Trafficking Law: Crackdown on Backpage, Changes by Reddit, Craigslists," *Speaker Paul Ryan's Press Office,* April 10, 2018. https://www.speaker.gov/general/new-trafficking-law-crackdown-backpagecom-changes-reddit-craigslist

110   Charlie Savage and Timothy Williams, "U.S. Seizes Backpage.com, a Site Accused of Enabling Prostitution," *New York Times*, April 7, 2018. https://www.nytimes.com/2018/04/07/us/politics/backpage-prostitution-classified.html?mtrref=undefined

111   John Villasenor, "Smartphones for the unbanked: How mobile money will drive digital inclusion in developing countries," *Brookings Institute*, September 2013. http://www.brookings.edu/~/media/research/files/papers/2013/09/16-smartphones-mobile-money-developing-countries-villasenor/brookingsmobilemoneyrevised-92313.pdf

112   WorldRemit. https://www.worldremit.com/

113   Mark Trevelyan, "UN Agency punished Somalia whistleblower," *Reuters,* May 9, 2010. http://www.reuters.com/article/2010/03/10/idUSLDE62900Z

114   Mfonobong Nsehe, "Somali Entrepreneur Raises $100 Million For Money Transfer Startup WorldRemit," *Forbes,* February 9, 2015.

http://www.forbes.com/sites/mfonobongnsehe/2015/02/19/somali-entrepreneur-raises-100-million-for-money-transfer-startup-worldremit/

115   Stephen Gyasi Jnr, "Ghana: How Susu evolved into microfinance," *African Business Magazine*, March 20, 2012. http://africanbusinessmagazine.com/uncategorised/ghana-how-susu-evolved-into-microfinance/

116   Iseult Ward "The Food Cloud Story," *stopfoodwaste*, June 9, 2015. https://www.youtube.com/watch?v=X3DlSyC5t94

117   Iseult Ward, "The Food Cloud Story," *stopfoodwaste*, June 9, 2015. https://www.youtube.com/watch?v=X3DlSyC5t94

118   "The problem," *FoodCloud.com* (with sources: United Nations organizations). https://food.cloud/the-problem/

119   "Malnutrition," World Health Organization, February 16, 2018, http://www.who.int/news-room/fact-sheets/detail/malnutrition.

120   Megan Gibson, "Want to Solve Hunger and Food Waste? She Made the App For That," *TIME,* November 14, 2014. http://time.com/collection-post/3583520/shareable-feast/

121   "What's Our Latest Figure in Surplus Food Redistribution? [Update]," FoodCloud, July 11, 2017. https://food.cloud/whats-our-latest-figure-in-surplus-food-redistribution-update/

122   Tim Ferriss, "The Tim Ferriss Show Transcripts: Brandon Stanton." *The Blog of Author Tim Ferriss*, June 27, 2018. https://tim.blog/2018/06/27/the-tim-ferriss-show-transcripts-brandon-stanton/

123   Tim Ferriss, "The Tim Ferriss Show Transcripts: Brandon Stanton." The Blog of Author Tim Ferriss, June 27, 2018. https://tim.blog/2018/06/27/the-tim-ferriss-show-transcripts-brandon-stanton/

124   "In 10,000 Snaps Of The Shutter, A 'Photographic Census' Of A City." *NPR,* October 24, 2015. www.npr.org/2015/10/24/451184837/in-10-000-snaps-of-the-shutter-a-photographic-census-of-a-city

125   Tim Ferriss, "The Tim Ferriss Show Transcripts: Brandon Stanton." The Blog of Author Tim Ferriss, June 27, 2018. https://tim.blog/2018/06/27/the-tim-ferriss-show-transcripts-brandon-stanton/

126   Tim Ferriss, "The Tim Ferriss Show Transcripts: Brandon Stanton." The Blog of Author Tim Ferriss, June 27, 2018. https://tim.blog/2018/06/27/the-tim-ferriss-show-transcripts-brandon-stanton/

127 Humans of New York Creator Brandon Stanton, "On How I Approach Strangers in the Street," MyUCD, Dublin." *YouTube,* April 24, 2014, www.youtube.com/watch?v=KPxzlGPrM3A

128 Humans of New York Creator Brandon Stanton, "On How I Approach Strangers in the Street," MyUCD, Dublin." *YouTube,* April 24, 2014. www.youtube.com/watch?v=KPxzlGPrM3A

129 "Hurricane Sandy: As It Happened." *WSJDigitalNetwork,* November 2, 2012. www.youtube.com/watch?v=KeaG1jRLIBw

130 "Cause of Breezy Point Fire During Sandy Determined." *NBC New York,* December 24, 2012. www.nbcnewyork.com/news/local/ Cause-Breezy-Point-Queens-Rockaway-Fires-During-Sandy- Determined-184715051.html

131 Steven Mufson, "3 Nuclear Power Reactors Shut down during Hurricane Sandy." *The Washington Post,* October 30, 2012. www.washingtonpost. com/business/economy/3-nuclear-power-reactors-shut-down-during- sandy/2012/10/30/7ddd3a94-22b6-11e2-8448-81b1ce7d6978_story. html?utm_term=.53e043e25439.

132 "Hurricane Sandy Fast Facts." *CNN,* October 19, 2017. www.cnn. com/2013/07/13/world/americas/hurricane-sandy-fast-facts/index.html

133 "Humans of New York and Tumblr fundraiser: Brandon Stanton's Photos Inspire Viral Campaign (Photos)," *Huffington Post,* November 20, 2012. https://www.huffingtonpost.com/2012/11/19/humans-of-new- york_n_2161537.html

134 Indiegogo.com https://www.indiegogo.com/about/what-we-do

135 Kelly Faircloth, "Hurricane Relief Goes Viral, With a Little Help From Tumblr and Indiegogo." *Observer,* Nov. 12, 2012. WWW.observer.com/2012/11/ humans-of-new-york-blog-tumblr-indiegogo-hurricane-sandy/

136 Tom Wrobleski, "Stephen Siller Foundation Ready to Hand out Money to Staten Island Hurricane Sandy Victims." *SILive.com,* December 16, 2012, www.silive.com/news/2012/12/stephen_siller_foundation_read.html.

137 Callie Schweitzer, "These are the 30 People under 30 changing the world," *TIME Magazine,* December 5, 2013. http://ideas.time. com/2013/12/06/these-are-the-30-people-under-30-changing-the-world/

138 Brandon Stanton, *Humans of New York: Stories,* (St. Martin's Press, 2015) https://www.amazon.com/Humans-New-York-Brandon-Stanton/dp/1250058902

139 Natasha Culzac, "Humans of New York: Photographic blog partners with UN for dispatches from Iraq," *The Independent,* August 11, 2014. https://www.independent.co.uk/news/world/middle-east/humans-of-new-york-photographic-blog-partners-with-un-for-dispatches-from-iraq-9662226.html

140 Tim Ferriss, "The Tim Ferriss Show Transcripts: Brandon Stanton." *The Blog of Author Tim Ferriss*, June 27, 2018, https://tim.blog/2018/06/27/the-tim-ferriss-show-transcripts-brandon-stanton/

141 PBS Stations to Air: 'Malaria: Fever Wars,'" *Kaiser Health News,* June 11, 2009. https://khn.org/morning-breakout/dr00036468/ See also at *Amazon.com* to purchase: https://www.amazon.com/Malaria-Fever-Wars-Malaria-Fever/dp/B000EOTV48

142 "Interview with Katherine Commale," *United Methodist Communications,* umc.org. https://www.youtube.com/watch?v=zSCZ72iAR8g

143 "About Malaria," *Centers for Disease Control and Prevention*, Last updated March 29, 2018, https://www.cdc.gov/malaria/about/

144 "Malaria: Key Facts," *World Health Organization,* June 11, 2018. http://www.who.int/en/news-room/fact-sheets/detail/malaria

145 "About us: We can be the generation to defeat malaria, *"NothingButNets. net.* https://nothingbutnets.net/about/

146 "Interview with Katherine Commale," *United Methodist Communications,* umc.org. https://www.youtube.com/watch?v=zSCZ72iAR8g

147 Donald G. McNeil Jr., "A $10 Mosquito Net is Making Charity Cool," *New York Times*, June 2, 2008. https://www.nytimes.com/2008/06/02/us/02malaria.html

148 Suzy, Keenan, "Katherine and Lynda Commale exceed initial goal of raising $100,000 for Nothing but nets." *NothingButNets. org.* August 1, 2009. https://nothingbutnets.net/press-releases/katherine-and-lynda-commale-exceed-initial-goal-of

149 Donald G. McNeil Jr., "A $10 Mosquito Net is Making Charity Cool," *New York Times*, June 2, 2008. https://www.nytimes.com/2008/06/02/us/02malaria.html

150 "Annual Letter from Bill Gates," *Bill and Melinda Gates Foundation*, 2011. https://docs.gatesfoundation.org/Documents/2011-annual-letter.pdf

151 There's also many economic reasons for the Great Firewall. Banning some foreign companies has proven very advantageous for Chinese tech companies like AliBaba and QQ that self-censor and share data with the Chinese government.

152 This is an official government estimate and may have been deliberately understated, even in 2013, much less today.https://www.cnn.com/2013/10/07/world/asia/china-internet-monitors/index.html

153 Among other things, the Chinese government fabricates social media posts to distract from undesirable issues/topics. See: https://gking.harvard.edu/50c

154 For example, as of the writing of this manuscript, the top story on the Dalai Lama available on China's leading search engine is entitled "Dalai Lama distorts picture about Tibet".http://english.jschina.com.cn/20322/201507/t2253352.shtml

155 Gady Epstein,"China's Social Network: Zuckerberg and Sina Chat Over the Great Firewall," *Forbes,* February 16, 2011. https://www.forbes.com/sites/gadyepstein/2011/02/16/chinas-social-network-zuckerberg-and-sina-chat-over-the-great-firewall/#7cd3305d181d

156 Ralph Jennings, "China Demands Companies Stop Calling Taiwan A Country. Here's What They'll Do," *Forbes*, January 17, 2018. https://www.forbes.com/sites/ralphjennings/2018/01/17/corporations-will-quickly-comply-as-china-pressures-them-to-stop-calling-taiwan-a-country/#6690dc6d9bf4

157 Stephen McDonell, "Why China censors banned Winnie the Pooh, "*BBC News China Blog*, July 17, 2017. https://www.bbc.com/news/blogs-china-blog-40627855

158 Timothy B. Lee, "Watch the John Oliver segment that got Oliver's name banned in China," *Ars Technica*, June 25, 2018. https://arstechnica.com/tech-policy/2018/06/china-bans-online-mention-of-john-oliver-after-he-mocks-chinas-president/

159 Benjamin Haas, "China bans Winnie the Pooh film after comparisons to President Xi," *The Guardian*, August 7, 2018. https://www.theguardian.com/world/2018/aug/07/china-bans-winnie-the-pooh-film-to-stop-comparisons-to-president-xi

160 Kerry Allen, "China cernsorship after Xi Jinping presidency extension proposal," *BBC News,* February 26, 2018. https://www.bbc.com/news/world-asia-china-43198404

161 Joseph A Cannataci, 'Report of the special rapporteur on theright to privacy' (UN- HRC, A/HRC/34/60, 7 March 2017) para 45. http://www.ohchr.org/Documents/Issues/Privacy/A_HRC_34_60_EN.docx

162 "Biography of Joe Cannataci, Special Rapporteur on the right to privacy," United Nations Human Rights Office of the High Commissioner.https://www.ohchr.org/EN/Issues/Privacy/SR/Pages/JoeCannataci.aspx

163 "Biography of Joe Cannataci, Special Rapporteur on the right to privacy," *United Nations Human Rights Office of the High Commissioner*. https://www.ohchr.org/EN/Issues/Privacy/SR/Pages/JoeCannataci.aspx

164 Oxford dictionary. Access online: https://en.oxforddictionaries.com/definition/autonomy

165 George Orwell, *1984*, (Martin Secker & Warburg Ltd, London, 1949), Chapter 2.

166 George Orwell, *1984*, (Martin Secker & Warburg Ltd, London, 1949), pp 220

167 George Orwell, *1984*, (Martin Secker& Warburg Ltd, London, 1949), Chapter 2.

168 Editors of Encyclopedia Britannica, "Berlin Wall, Berlin Germany," *Encyclopedia Britannica*. https://www.britannica.com/topic/Berlin-Wall

169 "East to West: The Great Balloon Escape," *TIME Magazine*, October 1, 1979. http://content.time.com/time/subscriber/article/0,33009,947451,00.html

170 By one estimate, there was, on average, one spy or informer for every 6.5 citizens in the country. See John O. Koehler, *Stasi: The Untold Story of the East German Secret Police*, (Westview Press, 1999). https://

archive.nytimes.com/www.nytimes.com/books/first/k/koehler-stasi.
html?_r=2

171   "Stasi police keep people in fear for 40 years," *The Telegraph*,
October 2008. https://www.telegraph.co.uk/news/worldnews/europe/
germany/3275905/Stasi-police-kept-East-Germans-in-fear-for-40-years.
html. See also: *Betrayal Has No Expiration Date at* ChristhardLäpple.
com. http://christhard-laepple.com/?m=200810

172   Brendan I. Koerner, "Inside the cyberattack that shocked the US
government," *Wired*, October 23, 2016. https://www.wired.com/2016/10/
inside-cyberattack-shocked-us-government/

173   https://www.wired.com/2015/07/
massive-opm-hack-actually-affected-25-million/

174   Selena Larson, "Every single Yahoo account was hacked—3 billion
in all," *CNN*, October 4, 2017. https://money.cnn.com/2017/10/03/
technology/business/yahoo-breach-3-billion-accounts/index.html

175   Owais Sultan, "Experian Hack Leads To Data Breach of T-Mobile
Customers," Hack Read, October 2, 2015. https://www.hackread.com/
experian-hack-t-mobile-beach/

176   Lorenzo Franceschi-Bicchierai, "Teen Who Hacked Ex-CIA Director
John Brennan Gets Sentenced to 2 Years of Prison," *Vice.com*,
April 20, 2018. https://motherboard.vice.com/en_us/article/pax87v/
kane-gamble-crackas-with-attitude-cwa-sentence-prison

177   Luke Graham, "Cybercrime costs the global economy $450 billion:
CEO," *CNBC*, February 7, 2017. https://www.cnbc.com/2017/02/07/
cybercrime-costs-the-global-economy-450-billion-ceo.html

178   Brendan Pierson, "Anthem to pay record $115 million to settle U.S.
lawsuits over data breach," *Reuters*, June 23, 2017. https://www.reuters.
com/article/us-anthem-cyber-settlement/anthem-to-pay-record-115-
million-to-settle-u-s-lawsuits-over-data-breach-idUSKBN19E2ML

179   Todd Spandgler, "Facebook Says Info on Up to 87 Million Users
Was 'Improperly' Shared With Cambridge Analytica: Social giant
outlines more steps to restrict flow of personal data in wake of
scandal," *Variety*, April 4, 2018. https://variety.com/2018/digital/news/
facebook-87-million-users-cambridge-analytica-leak-1202743952/

180   "Egypt's military clashes with protestors; 7 dead," *Associated Press/ CBS News*, December 16, 2011. https://www.cbsnews.com/news/ egypts-military-clashes-with-protesters-7-dead/

181   John Scott-Railton, Bill Marczak, Ramy Raoof, and Etienne Maynier, "NILE PHISH: Large-Scale Phishing Campaign Targeting Egyptian Civil Society," *TheCitizenLab*, February 2, 2017. https://citizenlab. ca/2017/02/nilephish-report/

182   John Scott-Railton, Bill Marczak, Ramy Raoof, and Etienne Maynier, "NILE PHISH: Large-Scale Phishing Campaign Targeting Egyptian Civil Society," *TheCitizenLab*, February 2, 2017. https://citizenlab. ca/2017/02/nilephish-report/

183   "Privacy is an entry point to all civil liberties and human rights," *CELS,* September 25, 2017. https://www.cels.org.ar/web/en/2017/09/ privacy-is-an-entry-point-to-all-civil-liberties-and-human-rights/

184   Letter to Enrique Pefia Nieto, President of Mexico," *R3D*, June 28, 2017. https://privacyinternational.org/sites/default/files/2017-12/PI-R3D%20 Joint%20Letter.pdf

185   Deji Bryce Olukotum, "Spyware in Mexico: an interview with Luis Fernando García of R3D Mexico," *Accessnow*, June 23, 2017. https://www.accessnow.org/ spyware-mexico-interview-luis-fernando-garcia-r3d-mexico/

186   Edmund Burke, *Reflections on the Revolution*, (Oxford World's Classics, Reissue Edition). www.amazon.com/ Reflections-Revolution-France-Oxford-Classics/dp/0199539022

187   The Universal Declaration of Human Rights, *United Nations.* www. un.org/en/universal-declaration-human-rights/index.html

ABOUT THE AUTHOR

Matthew Daniels, JD, PhD, was raised in poverty by a single mother in New York's Spanish Harlem. His family was forced onto welfare when his mother was assaulted by four men on the way home from work, leaving her permanently disabled. Dr. Daniels attended inner-city public schools in NYC until receiving a full scholarship to Dartmouth College. He went on to receive a Public Interest Scholarship to the University of Pennsylvania Law School and a fellowship to do his doctorate in American politics at Brandeis.

As the founder of the nonprofit educational organization Good of All, Dr. Daniels has launched several academic centers in three countries (US, UK, and Republic of Korea). His work has been endorsed by the Attorney General of UK & Wales, the former Lord Chancellor of the UK, the Martin Luther King Advisory Council, former members of the Constitutional Court of the Republic of Korea, South Korean human rights officials, the Chairman of the Homeland Security Advisory Council, two former Chairmen of the Joint Chiefs of Staff, the former Director of the FBI, and dozens of legal and academic experts around the world.

Dr. Daniels is the Creator and Executive Producer of the Human Rights Network (HRN), an educational video network promoting universal rights through digital media. HRN operates digital video channels in multiple languages with a combined audience of over twenty-five million.

Dr. Daniels has also developed the MLK Universal Rights Scholarship Program, in collaboration with the Martin Luther King Advisory Council of Georgia, focused on applying the universal rights principles championed by Dr. Martin Luther King Jr. to today's critical human rights issues. The program has been endorsed by civil rights pioneer Ambassador Andrew Young and awards annual scholarships to students at historically black colleges.

Dr. Daniels teaches human rights and the rule of law on three continents. He serves as Chair of Law & Human Rights at the Institute of World Politics in Washington, DC. He is the founder of the Center for Law and Digital Culture at Brunel Law School in London, England, and an Adjunct Professor of Law at Handong International Law School in Pohang, South Korea.

For more information please visit: www.humanliberty.org